High Impact Teacher's Guide

IELTS

ACADEMIC MODULE

Patrick Bourne

PEARSON
Longman

Preface

As *High Impact IELTS* is intended for students looking for a relatively high IELTS result, this book does not focus on the basics of the test. There is an answer key as well as guidelines and suggestions for teaching the lesson. Suggested answers are also given where appropriate. All of these areas are clearly identifiable throughout the *Teacher's Guide*.

In the back of the book (Appendix B) you will find a Task II writing guide. Using this will help you mark students' work and also allow students to identify areas of weakness.

The Listening tape scripts are all included in Appendix C.

The model answers to the essay tasks are included in Appendix D.

www.pearsoned.co.nz

Your comments on this book are welcome at
feedback@pearsoned.co.nz

Pearson Education New Zealand
a division of Pearson New Zealand Ltd
Corner Rosedale Road and Airborne Road
Albany, Auckland
New Zealand

Associated companies throughout the world

ISBN 0 582 54852 7

Produced by Pearson Education New Zealand
Printed in Malaysia, PA
Typeset in 10.5/12 Palatino

We use paper from sustainable forestry

Social issues

1

Unit 1.1   Skimming and scanning (reading)

GUIDELINE

1.1 EXERCISE **1** (page 1)

Reading any headings and then skimming the text is generally accepted as the first thing to do when the test begins. Students may have a different opinion (they may choose to read the questions first). Whatever approach is favoured, now is the best time to decide on which method to follow and stick to it throughout the course. The main aim of the question is to get students thinking about their approach to the test so their reaction becomes instinctive, saving valuable minutes of panic on the day of the test.

GUIDELINE

1.1 EXERCISE **2** (pages 1–2)

Some of the headings are based on vocabulary. Others are more obscure, such as 'Auckland on the right tracks' – a pun on new plans for a railway service.

ANSWER

1.1 EXERCISE **3** (page 2)

	Good idea	Bad idea
Reading the title	✔	
Reading every word		✔
Reading the first sentence of each paragraph	✔	
Underlining names (people, places, etc.)	✔	
Concentrating on difficult vocabulary		✔
Looking at illustrations	✔	

SUGGESTED ANSWER

1.1 EXERCISE **4** (pages 2–3)

This text is about the similarities and differences between approaches of two famous supporters of rights for African Americans.

GUIDELINE ANSWER

1.1 EXERCISE **5** (page 3)

'Children and the Net' is the best heading. A quick glance at the text may lead students to select 'Internet advertising' or 'Surfing the web', but they do not fully encapsulate what is given in the text.

1.1 EXERCISE 6 (page 4)

ANSWER

a century

b wrestle

c oppression

d Harlem/Memphis (students need to find only one)

e April

f reasoning

g (Students need to find only one of the following) ultimately, America, encouraging, eventual, integrating, integration, communities, motivated, philosophy, organising, demonstration, radically

h 7

1.1 EXERCISE 7 (page 4)

GUIDELINE ANSWER

Although this is a subject that will appear many times throughout the course, the main aim of this exercise is to get students thinking about alternative ways of expressing the same information (transformation). You should also spend a little time focusing on question words (when = time, where = place, etc.).

For the first part, the most important words should be *When …* and *Erasmus*, but also point out that *started* in the text has become *launched* in the question, and, when scanning, students should be aware of such transformation. The answer to the question is *1998*.

1.1 EXERCISE 8 (page 4)

ANSWER

1 June, 1997

2 (Students need to find only one of the following) They can play games, download screensavers, win T-shirts.

3 Social, legal, political

4 No

EXTENSION ACTIVITY

1 The two readings are not really used in depth, but you could get students to write more questions and have other students skim for the answers.

2 If these were titles to texts, what do you think the texts would be about?
The increasing burden of the elderly   Multicultural businesses work best
Rich and poor: the ever-widening divide   Not all charity begins at home

3 Quickly scan Reading Passage 2 and find the following.

		Answers
1	E-mail you don't want	junk
2	An adjective beginning with 'o'	objectionable
3	A phrase which means 'good for the family'	family-friendly
4	Another noun for 'drink'	beverage
5	Something you can download	screen saver
6	The longest word	communications
7	The number of times cigarette (or cigarettes) is mentioned	3

Unit 1.2   Linking words (Task I & II)

GUIDELINE

This section is a little unusual as it focuses more on Task II than Task I, although linking words are important for both tasks. Linking words are such an important part of the test that they need to be studied early in order to become a natural part of their writing, and also to give you time to correct any errors.

1.2 EXERCISE 1 (page 4)

GUIDELINE

This should be a simple exercise for students to complete. Don't dwell on it too much, as *Exercise 2* explains that these are just simple examples.

ANSWER

Unemployment is increasing	*yet*	the government is not reacting.
	so	social welfare costs are rising.
	because	of the depressed economy.

ANSWER

1.2 EXERCISE 2 (page 5)

a Illegal immigrants continue to arrive in the country <u>in spite of</u> stricter government measures.

b <u>In addition to</u> having a lot of money, he is very good-looking.

c The level of English continues to be a problem amongst migrant workers. <u>As a result</u>, many companies have begun insisting on an IELTS result of at least 6.0.

d Building a road here will destroy an area of great natural beauty. <u>Furthermore</u>, nobody is really in support of it.

e <u>Not only</u> is the tourist situation deteriorating, it is <u>also</u> spreading to other industries.

ANSWER

1.2 EXERCISE 3 (page 5)

Time	in the meantime / meanwhile / while
Comparison	likewise / in the same way / equally
Contrast	whereas / in contrast / on the other hand / nevertheless
Example	for example / for instance / to illustrate
Cause/effect	consequently / hence / thus / as a result
Concession	although it may be true / granted / admittedly
Sequence	following which / subsequently / afterwards
Addition	moreover / furthermore / as well / in addition / not only … (but) also

1.2 EXERCISE 4 (pages 5–6)

a Moreover

b while

c hence

d even though

e nevertheless / even so

f consequently

g even so / nevertheless

h in spite of

i whereas

j so

k yet

l in contrast

1.2 EXERCISE 5 (page 6)

This exercise should demonstrate that linking words are not simply interchangeable; sentences often have to be rearranged to suit different words.

a Children from low-income families often do not pursue further education, whereas children from higher-income families often stay in education to university level or beyond.

Children from low-income families often do not pursue further education. In contrast, children from higher-income families often stay in education to university level or beyond.

b An increasing number of marriages are ending in divorce. Consequently, many people are choosing not to get married.

An increasing number of marriages are ending in divorce, so many people are choosing not to get married.

c Even though the situation may be beyond repair, the government should try to resolve it.

The situation may be beyond repair. Even so, the government should try to resolve it.

d Many people still sunbathe for long periods of time while knowing the dangers.

Many people still sunbathe for long periods of time in spite of knowing the dangers.

In spite of knowing the dangers, many people still sunbathe for long periods of time.

e There is a global agreement to reduce the number of nuclear weapons. Nevertheless, governments still stockpile them.

There is a global agreement to reduce the number of nuclear weapons, yet governments still stockpile them.

f English is easy. Moreover, it is useful. Lots of people learn it.

English is easy and it is useful, hence lots of people learn it.

Exercises 6, 7 and *8* focus on a common error – the misuse of 'On the other hand' and 'In contrast'.

1.2 EXERCISE 6 (page 6)

a *Example 1.* Good is positive. Expensive is negative.
Example 2. Good is positive. Bad is negative.

b The subject is the same for *Example 1* (A).

c The subject is different for *Example 2* (A and B).

ANSWER

1.2 EXERCISE 7 (page 7)

A 1 On the other hand
  2 In contrast
B 1 On the other hand
  2 In contrast
C 1 In contrast
  2 On the other hand

ANSWER

1.2 EXERCISE 8 (page 7)

a On the other hand (the subject is 'education')

b In contrast (the subject in the first part is 'state-funded education'; the subject in the second part is 'private education')

SUGGESTED ANSWER

1.2 EXERCISE 9 (pages 7–8)

The linking words given are only suggestions. Other words can be used.

Over recent years, there has been a dramatic increase in international migration, often[a] *as a result of* political and economic pressures at home. As with many social issues, this has had both positive and negative effects, as can be seen in an analysis of both Sydney and Auckland.

In Sydney, there are many areas which have been shaped by the cultures of other nationalities and ethnic groups making Australia their new home. There is an area steeped in the culture and tradition of the Chinese[b] (*hence* the name Chinatown), an area which has become so famous it even has its own website!

With one quarter of the population being foreign immigrants, Auckland has[c] *therefore* become very cosmopolitan, with representatives of over 35 nations living and working in or around New Zealand's largest city.

For both cities, this migration has had many advantageous effects.[d] *For instance,* dazzling arrays of different cuisines are available, from Indian curries to Turkish kebabs.[e] *In addition* to food, such a multicultural mix exposes us to much more of a variety of different traditions, outlooks and languages.[f] *Consequently,* we gain a much wider understanding of international cultures.

[g] *However,* with so many different perspectives in relatively close confinement, there are bound to be problems. Cultural communities develop, sometimes isolating themselves and importing their own sense of tradition and belief at the expense of the traditions of their new country.[h] *Moreover,* racial suspicions can grow, often developing into tense situations

To conclude,[i] *despite* the inevitable pressures inherent in such a variety of cultures, both Sydney and Auckland[j] *nevertheless* remain good examples of cross-cultural toleration and understanding.

GUIDELINE

1.2 EXERCISE 10 (page 8)

As this is only Unit 1, it may be worth brainstorming as a class before getting the students to put some ideas on paper. Planning isn't studied until Unit 2.2 for Task I and Unit 3.5 for Task II but students should still make some effort to organise their points before they begin.

Unit 1.3   Your family

1.3 EXERCISE 1 (page 8)

Parents refers to mother and father, but *family* is a lot more open to include brothers, sisters, etc. You may want to elicit a definition of 'relative' in preparation for Unit 1.6.

The Point of Impact that follows *Exercise 1* is important. Some students rehearse their answers to Part One questions so often that they stop listening accurately to the examiner, and answer the question they think they were asked but not the one they were actually asked. It is important to impress upon the students that they should listen carefully.

1.3 EXERCISE 2 (page 8)

Focus here on making sure your students realise that in English, family does not include distant relatives, friends or neighbours.

1.3 EXERCISE 3 (page 8)

For this exercise, read the following passage.

> Mary met Tom three years ago when she was visiting her friend Paul. When Mary came back to live in the city, Tom came too and they got married a year later. She introduced him to her brother John, but they haven't really become friends. Tom and Sid, Mary's father, get on well though – they go fishing together sometimes, and Sid's wife, Nancy, sometimes goes with them. Last year, Mary and Tom had a baby – a boy called Joshua. John and Eleanor were pleased, as their boy, David, now has a cousin to play with. I don't know if Tom's very happy though. I think he wants to go back to Christchurch. He says he hasn't got any real friends here, apart from Mary's friend Jeff.

Mary's immediate family	Mary's extended family	Other
John (brother)	Eleanor (sister-in-law)	Jeff (friend)
Sid (father)	David (nephew)	Paul (friend)
Nancy (mother)		
Joshua (son)		
Tom (husband)		

1.3 EXERCISE 4 (page 9)

You might want students to write the names and relationships of people into columns as in *Exercise 3* before they begin.

1.3 EXERCISE 5 (page 9)

Remind students that some adjectives describing character are positive or negative depending on your own point of view. These adjectives should be written in the 'neutral' column.

ANSWER

Positive	Neutral	Negative
caring, generous, open-minded, cheerful, hardworking, trustworthy, optimistic, sociable, attentive	ambitious, careful, spontaneous, sensitive, reserved	aggressive, selfish, impolite, impatient, moody, indecisive, lazy

1.3　EXERCISE 6　(page 9)

GUIDELINE

At this stage in the course, it may be a good idea to get students making a few short notes before they speak (avoid full sentences as students may end up reading rather than speaking). Once they have made some notes, you could get students in front of the class or talking in pairs.

EXTENSION ACTIVITY

Candidates could be asked to talk about family in Part One, Two or Three. Below are some Part Three extension questions that the interviewer could ask. You could ask students to think about any family-related extension questions that could come up in Part Three. Either with students' ideas or the questions below, you could elicit some possible answers in order to practise their brainstorming techniques.

1　How important do you think childhood is in shaping the adult we become?
2　Do you think that families have changed over the last XXXX years?
3　Do you think parenting has changed much over the last XXXX years?
4　How important do you think families are for individuals and society?
5　What do you think about the changing role of women in the family?

Unit 1.4　Personal information (listening)

1.4　EXERCISE 1　(page 10)

ANSWER

Personal information covers areas like name, surname, date of birth, etc. In the listening, this mostly comes when you need to complete a table, often as a form (complaint form, application, contract, etc.).

1.4　EXERCISE 2　(page 10)

GUIDELINE

After completing *Exercises 1* and *2*, you might want to get students 'interviewing' each other (in much the same way as in Unit 1.6).

1.4　EXERCISE 3　(page 10)

	Name	Place
a	Edmund Hillary	Auckland
b	Katherine Mansfield	Wellington
c	Alexander Aitken	Dunedin

	Name	Place
d	Te Rangi Hiroa	Wairarapa
e	Kate Sheppard	Liverpool
f	Ernest Rutherford	Brightwater
g	Colin Murdoch	Timaru
h	John Britten	Christchurch

1.4 EXERCISE 4 (page 10)

This is not really IELTS related and may be little more than guesswork, but it might give the previous exercise some context.

	Famous for being …	Who?
A	the inventor of the disposable syringe	Colin Murdoch
B	the first man to climb Everest	Edmund Hillary
C	a revolutionary motorcycle designer	John Britten
D	a 19th-century writer and poet	Katherine Mansfield
E	the leader of the women's suffrage movement	Kate Sheppard
F	a brilliant mathematician	Alexander Aitken
G	a Maori doctor, politician and anthropologist	Te Rangi Hiroa
H	the first man to split the atom	Ernest Rutherford

1.4 EXERCISE 5 (page 11)

Extension questions are often after the personal information questions. In this example, questions 7, 8, 9 and 10 are all extension questions.

1.4 EXERCISE 6 (page 11)

1	Jane Kinsella	6	4
2	British	7	Business Studies
3	Maich Road	8	Savings
4	021 455 7326	9	a friend
5	Unemployed	10	Admissions Office

1.4 EXERCISE 7 (page 11)

The following are only potential suggestions.

Paid Leave Application	Video Supreme Rentals	Bevis Rent-a-Car
How long?	Membership fee	Driving licence
Purpose?	Name and address?	Credit card
Starting from?	Proof of address	Insurance
Return date?	Late fee	Damage waiver?
Contact number?	Overdue fines	Engine size?
		Mileage
		Type of vehicle?

READING

ANSWER

1.4 EXERCISE 8 (page 12)

1	James Bartolo	6	£4000
2	01/08/73	7	None
3	146 Eastern Road	8	3
4	Yes	9	Aitken
5	Ford Laser	10	£275

Unit 1.5 Brainstorming

GUIDELINE

The Point of Impact that opens this section is perhaps the most important of the Task II tips.

1.5 EXERCISE 1 (page 12)

GUIDELINE

Before opening the book, you might want to write the title on the board and get students to think of at least some of the points that are mentioned in *Exercise 1*. Don't be too concerned if students can't think of any more points, but accept anything at this point even if you feel the connection to the topic is tenuous.

1.5 EXERCISE 2 (page 13)

GUIDELINE

As students brainstorm for ideas, encourage them to take notes as they will be referring back to this work. You might find it easier with small groups to focus on just one question.

1.5 EXERCISE 3 (page 13)

SUGGESTED ANSWER

e.g. shopaholics, socialise too much, lazy, lose their money gambling …
Remind students that they are only required to write 250 words, which does not leave room for tenuously connected ideas.

1.5 EXERCISE 4 (page 13)

SUGGESTED ANSWER

In addition to these points, students may have added ideas of their own.

Their fault

rich people have earned their money

welfare payments in some countries

some people do not have the ability to save

Not their fault

difficult to break out of a generational cycle of poverty

those unable to work/earn

government should distribute wealth equally

location of country can lead to limited development opportunities

economy causes rich/poor gap

harsh government policies

inheritance

depends on education

1.5 EXERCISE 5 (page 14)

Exercise 4 divided the essay. The following ideas allow students to structure each paragraph.

Personal	Political	Environmental
Their fault: rich people have always earned money some people do not have the ability to save	Their fault: welfare payments in some countries	Their fault:
Not their fault: difficult to break out of a generational cycle of poverty those unable to work/earn	Not their fault: government should distribute equally harsh government policies	Not their fault: economy causes rich/poor gap location of country can lead to limited development opportunities

1.5 EXERCISE 6 (page 14)

These exercises need to be closely monitored, as they will vary greatly depending on how the lesson has progressed.

GUIDELINE

1.5 EXERCISE 7 (page 14)

You are looking for students to produce an essay with clearly defined ideas. At this point it is not overly important that they write 250 words.

GUIDELINE

EXTENSION ACTIVITY

Brainstorm responses to the following statements.
There is no excuse for unemployment. There are enough jobs for everyone.
The woman's role is in the home.
Failing is proof that you didn't try hard enough.
With proper study, everyone should achieve 100% exam success.

Unit 1.6   Getting ideas

A possible introduction could be a short game of word association. One student says a word, and the next student has three seconds to think of a related word. This continues around the room until a student repeats an idea, takes more than three seconds or uses a word with no easily definable connection to the previous word.

This then leads into the Point of Impact in the student's book.

GUIDELINE

1.6 EXERCISE 1 (page 14)

There are a number of different areas students could brainstorm for this exercise. At this point in the course, it is important that students begin producing full and extended answers. They should also be using some of the skills presented in Unit 1.5.

GUIDELINE

GUIDELINE

1.6 EXERCISE 2 (page 15)

You might want to make this exercise something of a grammar review, getting students to produce sentences using as many different forms of grammar as possible.

Unit 1.7   **Headings**

GUIDELINE

An important part of this lesson is reviewing the skills presented in Unit 1.1 (skimming). You might want to begin with a brief review.

You could start this lesson off by writing CONTROVERSIAL on the board, getting students to brainstorm for subjects that are causing some controversy. Current examples could include nuclear power. You could put students on to more of the right track by leading them onto SCIENCE and CONTROVERSY.

1.7 EXERCISE 1 (page 15)

ANSWER

		True	False
A	There are always more headings than paragraphs.	✔	
B	There are never more than five paragraphs.		✔
C	Some of the headings are similar.	✔	
D	At least one word from the heading can always be matched in the text.		✔
E	The same heading is used more than once.		✔
F	If you are given an example, it will always be the first paragraph.		✔

1.7 EXERCISE 2 (page 15)

ANSWER

a   Disappointment in GM foods (seemed to be/truth [is] different/not the solution … promised).

1.7 EXERCISE 3 (page 15)

GUIDELINE
SUGGESTED
ANSWER

Students should consider headings as short summaries of what the paragraph is presenting. Suggestion: Mistrust of artificial harvests.

Before you begin the next exercise, draw students' attention to points 1 and 2 from the Point of Impact – they will be applying these points in the next two exercises.

1.7 EXERCISE 4 (pages 16–17)

The following are just some of the key points students could note.

SUGGESTED
ANSWER

Paragraph A: sprayed to kill everything
                 decline in farmland wildlife
                 decrease in food supplies

Paragraph B: grown for only one year
                 farmland ecology is poorly understood
                 wildlife never studied before
                 soil types may vary

Paragraph C:　many years/over 50 years to discover
　　　　　　　persists for up to two years/for at least 10 years
　　　　　　　long after monitoring has stopped

Paragraph D:　livelihood of other farmer
　　　　　　　beekeepers…will be forced to move
　　　　　　　this will affect land values

Paragraph E　nature is already evolving
　　　　　　　develop…tolerance
　　　　　　　adapt as natural crops

1.7 EXERCISE 5 (page 17)

ANSWER

Paragraph A	v	Paragraph D	iv
Paragraph B	ii	Paragraph E	vii
Paragraph C	i		

Unit 1.8　Reading graphs

At the end of this lesson, students will be writing a Task I essay. This is the first time students have attempted to write a complete essay.

GUIDELINE

1.8 EXERCISE 1 (page 18)

ANSWER

a　✗ – The graph does not talk about per cent, it refers to life expectancy.

b　✗ – The graph refers to 'average' not 'all'.

c　✗ – We are not given any statistics regarding population numbers.

d　✔

1.8 EXERCISE 2 (page 18)

ANSWER

a　The graph actually refers to people, though students often get confused and talk about the number of houses.

b　Years over a 20-year period.

c　Number of people (homeowners) in thousands.

1.8 EXERCISE 3 (page 19)

It is very important that students are clear about how to complete the next two exercises, as mistakes become increasingly difficult to correct as students progress through the course.

GUIDELINE

ANSWER

upward	downward	even
to increase (v)	a fall (n)	to remain steady (v)
a rise (n)	to decrease (v)	to level off (v)
to improve (v)	to decline (v)	a plateau (n)
to climb (v)	to deteriorate (v)	
to recover (v)	a drop (n)	
	to plummet (v)	
	to plunge (v)	

1.8 EXERCISE 4 (page 19)

SUGGESTED
ANSWER

Columns B and E appear to be very subjective. Some teachers/students may have different opinions.

adjectives			adverbs		
a	b	c	d	e	g
dramatic sharp abrupt rapid	marked significant moderate	marginal gradual slight	sharply dramatically abruptly rapidly	moderately significantly markedly	gradually marginally slightly

Before moving on to the next exercise, you might want to get students to refer back to *Exercise 1* and very quickly check that they can differentiate between verbs and nouns.

ANSWER

1.8 EXERCISE 5 (pages 19–20)

The description	The graph	The description	The graph
(X) fluctuated There were fluctuations in (X) (X) was erratic	D	(X) fell dramatically There was a dramatic fall in (X) (X) plunged	L
(X) reached a peak (X) peaked	A	(X) recovered dramatically There was an abrupt rise in (X) (X) soared	B
(X) reached a plateau (X) levelled off	G	There was a slight decrease in (X) There was a slight fall in (X) (X) fell slightly in …	C
(X) remained constant	H	There was a slight increase in (X) There was a slight rise in (X) (X) rose slightly in …	J
There was an upward trend in (X) Overall, (X) increased	K	There was a steady decline in (X) (X) declined steadily There was a moderate decline in (X)	I
There was a downward trend in (X) Overall, (X) decreased	F	There was a steady recovery in (X) (X) recovered steadily There was a moderate increase in (X)	E

1.8 EXERCISE 6 (page 21)

GUIDELINE

As this is only the first unit, don't expect students to be able to write a perfect Task I. It is a good idea if possible to put the graph on an overhead projector, allowing the entire class to focus on it together. This means you can pool your students' ideas. As later units teach further skills for Task I, you are only looking for the basics in this exercise. Your students may well not reach the 150-word limit, but you can use what they write as an indication of what areas will need to be concentrated on in the future.

Unit 1.9   Beginning Part Three

This section is similar to Unit 1.5, in that it covers brainstorming for ideas. However, these ideas should then be turned into questions that could be used in Part Three.

GUIDELINE

1.9   EXERCISE 1   (page 21)

Do you think we are becoming too materialistic?
Do you believe we attach more importance to objects as we get older?
Do you think the objects we treasure most are given to us in our childhood?

SUGGESTED ANSWER

1.9   EXERCISE 2   (page 22)

In later units students will be introduced to more detailed steps. Until then you should get students to consider their answers using these points whenever the situation arises.

GUIDELINE

Unit 1.10   Short-answer questions (listening)

1.10   EXERCISE 1   (page 22)

a Sydney Mardi Gras   b January   c Over one million

ANSWER

1.10   EXERCISE 2   (page 22)

a What / festival   b When / start   c How many / people

ANSWER

1.10   EXERCISE 3   (page 22)

a	Who	person
b	When	time/date
c	Where	place
d	Why	reason
e	What	thing
f	Which	one person/thing from a limited number
g	How	explanation
h	How many	number
i	How often	frequency

SUGGESTED ANSWER

1.10   EXERCISE 4   (page 23)

a Overpopulation   d Poor sanitation
b Mexico City   e The international community
c 20 million

ANSWER

SPEAKING SPEAKING SPEAKING

READING & LISTENING READING & LISTENING READING

1.10 REVIEW   The listening in this section is very similar to Unit 1.4 *Exercise 6* as it reviews the skills taught so far.

ANSWER

a Hawberry	f Secretary
b 22 May	g Business
c 26	h Gets full quickly
d 714 721	i International Marketing
e No mobile phone	j Admissions (department)

Unit 1.11   Academic writing

1.11 EXERCISE 1   (pages 23–24)

ANSWER

Paragraph A – in the wrong register.
Paragraph B – the sentences are too short (they need to be more complex).
Paragraph C – the punctuation is wrong.

1.11 EXERCISE 2   (page 24)

ANSWER

Description	Written in a formal style, presenting both facts and opinions	Written in a formal style, presenting facts	Written in an informal style, presenting opinions	Written in a neutral style, presenting facts	Written in a neutral style, presenting opinions
Text	C	D	A	B	E

You might find it useful to elicit what makes the texts formal, informal or neutral as a review of *Exercises 2* and *3*.

1.11 EXERCISE 3   (page 25)

SUGGESTED ANSWER

Students may have other (suitable) answers to those given.
A A letter or e-mail between friends (students).
B A guide book .
C A letter to a tour operator or hotel.
D An e-mail from an IELTS testing centre to a potential candidate.
E A restaurant guide review.

1.11 EXERCISE 4   (page 25)

ANSWER

Sentence b is superior (a non-defining relative clause makes a more complex sentence, as explained in the Point of Impact that follows).

1.11 EXERCISE 5   (page 25)

ANSWER

a defining	d defining
b non-defining	e non-defining
c defining	

1.11 EXERCISE 6 (page 25)

This exercise is designed to check whether students are aware of the grammar of relative clauses. It is not a grammar presentation, so if students have difficulty with this exercise then you could consider a separate lesson on this area.

GUIDELINE

a America, which is one of the world's most developed countries, gives millions of dollars in aid to developing nations every year. (commas)

ANSWER

b Students **who** communicate with their classmates in English often become considerably more fluent and confident.

c We should, of course, punish those **who** break the law.

d The population is increasing, **which** is putting strain on both the environment and our supply of natural resources.

1.11 EXERCISE 7 (page 26)

There are many reasons to ban personal ownership of guns. A major reason why governments should not allow people to have guns is because of the potential for accidents. In America, for example, you can legally shoot people if you find them robbing your house, but this can lead to people dying over cases of mistaken identity. In addition, there are crimes where people act rashly or in anger, so guns which were intended for defence are often used aggressively.

SUGGESTED ANSWER

EXTENSION ACTIVITY

You could get students to complete the essay in *Exercise 7* using some opposing ideas and adding a conclusion.

Unit 1.12   Topic Card: Social issues

Using the topic card

The last section of Units 1–8 end by using a topic card related to the theme of each unit. When basing the lesson around a topic card, it is important to use as many different techniques as possible. Here are some suggestions:

GUIDELINE

* Record pairs of students practising an interview as interviewer and candidate. Have them play the recordings back and self-correct.

* Have a pair of students holding the interview as interviewer and candidate in front of the class, with the rest of the class taking notes.

* Have pairs of students practise the interview as interviewer and candidate, with the 'interviewer' making notes.

* Split the class into two teams, each team working in cooperation as a single candidate. The teacher asks the questions in the role of the interviewer and both teams have time to formulate their replies. For the topic card, they prepare their speech and then select a speaker. The teacher awards points throughout for good responses.

Be careful when recording or getting students to act in the class, as some students can be very sensitive.

SPEAKING SPEAKING SPEAKING

1.12 EXERCISE 1 (page 26)

GUIDELINE

Students should consider some relevant vocabulary for each prompt, but focus on positive adjectives of character/personality: kind, generous, warm-hearted, etc.

1.12 EXERCISE 2 (page 26)

SUGGESTED ANSWER

Possible extension questions:

How important do you think it is to have friends?

Has modern technology such as the Internet caused us to lose our social skills?

What is your opinion on Internet dating?

Is it easy to make friends in your country?

1.12 EXERCISE 3 (page 26)

Refer to the teacher's notes at the beginning of Unit 1.12.

2
Life and leisure

Unit 2.1 Unknown vocabulary (reading)

Vocabulary is often the biggest difficulty a student faces in the IELTS exam. In this section, there are five pointers to help with new vocabulary (context, contrast, explanation, word groups and logic), as well as prefixes and suffixes. It is worth encouraging students (if they don't do so already) to write new vocabulary into a notebook.

Before you move to the lesson, you could try brainstorming for any techniques students know for dealing with unknown vocabulary.

2.1 EXERCISE 1 (page 27)

This leads well into the Point of Impact but make sure students realise that these words are made up.

Go through the five points as a class; when you get to point 4 (word groups), you may want to take them back to *Exercise 1* and distinguish the word groups.

2.1 EXERCISE 2 (pages 27–28)

The answers are given at the end of the exercise in the students' book.

2.1 EXERCISE 3 (pages 28–29)

The aim of the lesson is simply to apply the strategies in any form. It is not that important if students are unable to identify exactly which pointer helped most.

A Hooligans (pointer 2 – contrast) = not well-behaved fans/*do* intend to cause trouble

B Thermal (pointer 5 – logic) = clothing/skiing (logically must be connected with keeping warm)

C Pilates (pointer 3 – explanation) = a form of exercise

D Impoverished (pointer 4 – word groups) = something that prevents overseas holidays or modern toys

E Avalanches (pointer 1 – context) = something bad when climbing mountains

2.1 EXERCISE 4 (pages 29–30)

Students should not be expected to give such full definitions. For number 3, for example, the text suggests only that it is some kind of sporting event.

1 An international sporting event.	2 Unconnected to religious matters.
3 A sporting event involving a long spear-like stick.	4 To give someone something to show respect.
5 Caused a feeling or situation to exist.	6 A place with an open area to watch

GUIDELINE GUIDELINE GUIDELINE GUIDELINE SUGGESTED ANSWER ANSWER

READING & LISTENING READING & LISTENING READING & LISTENING

7	The most important factor.		8	With people or society's best interests at heart.
9	Strange or amusing because misplaced or unexpected.		10	A period of 1000 years.
11	Suitable or right for the occasion.		12	Damaged the reputation of something.

2.1 REVIEW (pages 30–31)

ANSWER

1	iv		7	three (Paragraph E)
2	ix		8	the Romans invaded (Paragraph D)
3	ii		9	(the god) Zeus (Paragraph A)
4	vii		10	no (Paragraph C)
5	i		11	5 days (Paragraph D)
6	v		12	nearly 200 (Paragraph F)

EXTENSION ACTIVITY

Students could apply the five vocabulary skills to earlier passages of the book or from other sources (newspapers, etc.).

Unit 2.2   Preparing a plan for Task I

The first part of this sections reviews 'Reading graphs' (Unit 1.8).

2.2 EXERCISE 1 (page 31)

**GUIDELINE
ANSWER**

If you have available resources, it is a good idea to use an overhead projector for the first part of the unit. It focuses the class in one direction and makes eliciting information easier. The first thing students should do is make sure they know what they are looking at by following the three points given in the Point of Impact after *Exercise 5* in Unit 1.8.

2.2 EXERCISE 2 (page 31)

ANSWER

It should be very simple for students to recognise that this is the same graph divided by sex and now with a past time (1999).

2.2 EXERCISE 3 (page 32)

GUIDELINE

For this exercise, elicit as much information from your students as you can. Don't feel that you have to get students to predict everything that makes up the plan on the next page, as long as they are at least on the right lines. Answers are given in the Point of Impact that follows.

ANSWER

2.2 EXERCISE 4 (page 33)

1 Topic words?	most popular sports/watch/different age groups/average European city
2 Tense?	present
3 Axes?	per cent/three age ranges (15–25, 26–40, 41+) /six sports (soccer, tennis, golf, rugby, athletics, cricket)/people in 1000s

4 About?	percentage of different age ranges watching different sports
5 Trend(s)?	soccer, tennis and cricket show the same trend – rising with age
	soccer is the closest for all ages groups; no young people watch golf

2.2 EXERCISE 5 (page 33)

The main aim of this exercise is to ensure that students have applied the essentials of the lesson and incorporated them into the task. They should also be recycling the language that has already been presented.

GUIDELINE

Unit 2.3   Hobbies and interests

You could begin by creating a mind map to brainstorm topics related to 'life and leisure'. This could include sports, holidays, living abroad or life at home.

GUIDELINE

2.3 EXERCISE 1 (page 34)

1 What sports do you enjoy?

2 What sports are you interested in?

3 Do you like any particular sport?

4 What is your favourite sport?

5 Are you interested in any sports?

6 Do you have any interest in anything energetic?

7 Do you pursue any energetic pastimes?

SUGGESTED ANSWER

2.3 EXERCISE 2 (page 34)

a The reply is too short and needs to be expanded.

b The brief exercise on adjective endings is intended only to highlight a potential weakness. If students are confused about the answer, you should consider a separate grammar lesson.

GUIDELINE ANSWER

2.3 EXERCISE 3 (page 34)

The answers can be different, but only if the student can justify his or her opinion.

Rugby – energetic   Skydiving – exhilarating   Bowls – relaxing

SUGGESTED ANSWER

2.3 EXERCISE 4 (page 34)

As with *Exercise 3*, students need to justify answers. You may also want to add some other sports to the list.

GUIDELINE

2.3 EXERCISE 5 (page 34)

Make sure students do not choose one of the three sports given in *Exercises 3* and *4*.

GUIDELINE

2.3 EXERCISE 6 (page 34)

You can use any of the ideas given in Unit 1.12 ('Using the topic card') to complete this exercise.

GUIDELINE

WRITING WRITING SPEAKING SPEAKING SPEAKING SPEAKING SPEAKING

Unit 2.4   Predicting/anticipating (listening)

GUIDELINE

This lesson is intended to get students to carefully and productively use the time they have to read the questions before the listening begins. The first exercise begins with personal information – a subject students should be familiar with from Units 1.4 and 1.10.

2.4 EXERCISE 1 (page 35)

There is no recording for this exercise, but students should still be able to predict the following:

SUGGESTED ANSWER

 a This is probably a surname.

 b This is probably a house name or number.

 c This is probably a place name.

 d This is probably a phone number.

 e A period of time, probably in months or years.

 f There are three types of membership. Full membership probably includes the gym, the swimming pool and at least one other thing. The answer is one of the three choices given.

 g Expect to hear things like 'in the newspaper' or 'from a friend'.

2.4 EXERCISE 2 (page 35)

GUIDELINE

Remind students that although they may have predicted the type of answer, they should still remain open-minded. Students should be able to predict the following types of answers for questions 1–5.

ANSWER

 a length of time
 b number
 c income / length of course / course taken
 d name
 e place / room / location

2.4 EXERCISE 3 (page 36)

ANSWER

 a 10 weeks   d Mike Edwards
 b 8 students   e town hall
 c income

2.4 EXERCISE 4 (page 36)

GUIDELINE ANSWER

The idea of looking for differences is one that will be practised in more detail in Unit 2.10 (Multiple choice). This is just a basic introduction and a reminder that illustrations do sometimes appear in the listening test, and that predicting what you may hear is an essential skill. There is no tape for this exercise, but you could read the following description to students after they have noted the differences. It describes illustration B.

For the most powerful golfing shot, the club should be able to swing over 270 degrees. One leg should be almost straight and the other bent at the knee. It is important to keep your eye on the ball.

2.4 REVIEW (page 36)

Students should be able to predict some of the information, based on logic and the direction of earlier questions. It is also a review of Unit 1.10 (short-answer questions). They should also look closely at key words (including question words).

GUIDELINE

ANSWER

1 women's (lifestyles)
2 dishwashers and microwaves
3 leisure (pursuits)
4 more demanding

5 unnecessary goods
6 young professionals
7 environmental damage
8 moderation

Unit 2.5 Topic and task words

2.5 EXERCISE 1 (page 37)

The main focus of the essay will be in the second section 'Therefore the working week should be reduced'. This is explained in the Point of Impact that follows.

ANSWER

2.5 EXERCISE 2 (page 37)

The question should now read:

Point 1 – Advances in technology and automation have reduced the need for manual labour.

Point 2 – Therefore working hours should be reduced.

Point 3 – To what extent do you agree?

ANSWER

2.5 EXERCISE 3 (pages 37–38)

ANSWER

	Point 1	Point 2	Point 3
a	High-salary jobs often include free health insurance as part of an employment contract.	Private medical insurance is unfair, as it offers preferential treatment to the wealthy.	Do you agree?
b	The number of elderly people in the world is increasing.	This will lead to a number of social and medical problems.	To what extent do you agree?
c	Computer games have become the primary source of entertainment for most young children.	So children are not forming traditional social skills.	What can be done to reverse this trend?

2.5 EXERCISE 4 (page 38)

ANSWER

Do you agree or disagree? – suggests that no sensible argument can be based on entirely disagreeing with the proposition. *To what extent do you agree?* – suggests the candidate is free to entirely disagree if he/she chooses to do so.

2.5 EXERCISE 5 (page 38)

SUGGESTED ANSWER

Student answers may vary slightly.

    a topic = medical treatment because of addiction

    b topic = euthanasia is a right

    c topic = Government-provided medical care and old people

    d topic = we are becoming obsessed with diet

2.5 EXERCISE 6 (page 38)

ANSWER

    a Should they be treated?   **c** To what extent do you agree?

    b What is your opinion?   **d** Suggest possible reasons why.

2.5 EXERCISE 7 (page 39)

SUGGESTED ANSWER

    1 Is private medical insurance unfair because it gives preferential treatment to the wealthy?

    2 To what degree will the rising number of elderly people lead to social and medical problems?

    3 Can anything be done to stop children losing their social skills because of computer games?

2.5 REVIEW (page 39)

GUIDELINE

This exercise should review what students studied in Unit 1.5.

Unit 2.6   Preparing notes

GUIDELINE

A good way to start this lesson could be to tell students a short story, getting them to make notes as you talk. The subject is not really important but would be more appropriate if it was related to the unit theme of Life and Leisure. After you have finished, you could get students to try to retell the story, showing them the value of making clear notes.

2.6 EXERCISE 1 (page 39)

SUGGESTED ANSWER

favourite leisure activity	when/first
what	why/important
how often	

2.6 EXERCISE 2 (page 39)

GUIDELINE

What you are mainly looking for in your students is for them to be accurate and to the point. Encourage them to concentrate on the basics of what they want to say by making only bullet-point notes, not complete sentences, as explained in the Point of Impact that follows.

2.6 EXERCISE 3 (page 39)

Again make sure your students are not writing complete sentences. You may want to time them (they are only given one minute in the test).

GUIDELINE

2.6 EXERCISE 4 (page 39)

Make sure you check what the students are going to write notes about before they begin. You may want to quickly brainstorm appropriate topics around the class before you begin this activity so that students are all on the same wavelength.

GUIDELINE

2.6 EXERCISE 5 (page 39)

As with every speaking lesson, take advantage of this exercise to monitor students in pronunciation, intonation and confidence.

GUIDELINE

EXTENSION ACTIVITY

A useful extension to this exercise is to make notes on a short newspaper article and then speak about it to the class. This could be something students do at home ready for the next lesson, or you could take some articles into the class with you.

Unit 2.7 Text completion (reading)

2.7 EXERCISE 1 (page 40)

This exercise highlights the three different types of text-completion question. The types are defined in the Point of Impact that precedes the exercise.

GUIDELINE
ANSWER

  a (becoming) less significant   **b** Wall Street   **c** location

2.7 EXERCISE 2 (pages 40–41)

It may be a good idea to go through the first example with students, showing them that they need only get the essence of the text – it is not supposed to be a word-for-word transformation. There are no sample answers given as students may choose to do this a number of ways. The texts below are the same as the student's book, except that the essential information is given in bold.

GUIDELINE

A For John Taylor, an Auckland businessman, the day starts like any other. He gets up at 7.00 a.m., showers, shaves and has a light breakfast before heading to work – and it is here that Mr Taylor is **a little unusual**. Like an **increasing number of business professionals**, Mr Taylor has found that, armed with a notebook computer and an Internet connection, he can be just as **productive at home as he could in the city**.

B The **benefits** of the home office are largely **time related**. Whether stuck in a traffic jam or a crowded train, **commuting** to and from work can be **time consuming and irritating**. Working at **home**, you can **start work immediately** and with much **more flexibility**. Many people can **tailor their working day** around their **most productive hours**: a perfect **solution** for **those whose mornings are spent in a daze or for those who wind down in the early afternoon**. The **flexibility of working hours** also allows busy **professionals to work around other commitments**, especially **family** ones.

C Strangely enough, it is this very **flexibility** that can **cause stress**. Working **at home**, the pressure **is constant**. Physically, the **office is never left** and, therefore, many people also find that they **cannot mentally detach themselves** from their work. Working **alone** allows a certain degree of **independence** but the **lack of social interaction** means that working at home can be a **lonely** experience.

SPEAKING SPEAKING SPEAKING READING & LISTENING READING & LISTENING READING

2.7 EXERCISE 3 (page 41)

ANSWER

The *key words* are in *italics*, the **answers** (from the text) are in **bold.**

1 Without *office technology* we couldn't **work from home**.

2 With *fewer requirements for space*, businesses **reduce costs**.

3 Despite *political pressure*, public transport is still **unpopular**.

4 The *social aspects* of *working in an office* must not be **overlooked**.

2.7 EXERCISE 4 (page 41)

ANSWER

5 conduct business

6 financial

7 flexibility

8 benefits

9 psychological

ANSWER

2.7 REVIEW (page 41)

10	Paragraph A	i	13	Paragraph D	ix
11	Paragraph B	iv	14	Paragraph E	ii
12	Paragraph C	vii	15	Paragraph F	x

EXTENSION ACTIVITY

Although students have not practised many other question types at this point, they could write some scanning questions to ask a partner.

Unit 2.8 Writing an introduction to Task I

2.8 EXERCISE 1 (page 43)

SUGGESTED ANSWER

We can see that this is an introduction because it gives a brief summary of the graph. It is correct in that it does provide an overall description and first impression ('It's really interesting'), but there are a number of errors.

2.8 EXERCISE 2 (page 43)

GUIDELINE

The weaknesses are highlighted in *Exercise 3*.

2.8 EXERCISE 3 (page 43)

ANSWER

		Good idea	Bad idea
a	Vocabulary like *really interesting*		✔
b	Rephrasing the words from the graph (... *injuries connected to sport* ...)	✔	
c	Giving a general overview of the graph (... *three distinct periods* ...)	✔	
d	Using the construction *I can see*		✔ (should be passive)
e	Giving the reader an indication of the essay's structure (... *as I will now explain* ...)	✔	

2.8 EXERCISE 4 (page 43)

The rules can become fairly complex for this structure. Briefly, if you use 'that' or an introductory phrase like 'As can be seen…', then you must also use another verb.

GUIDELINE

2.8 EXERCISE 5 (page 44)

a 1 and 3	**c** 3	**e** 2	**g** 1
b 3	**d** 2	**f** 3	

ANSWER

2.8 REVIEW (page 44)

Topic words?	days taken off work/stress-related illnesses/job/men/women
Tense?	past (1998)
Axes?	days per year/job
About?	the number of days men & women take off work due to stress-related illness
Trends?	men always higher/dangerous job means more days off

SUGGESTED ANSWER

2.8 EXERCISE 6 (page 44)

Students should include all the positive points from *Exercise 3* in their introductions.

EXTENSION ACTIVITY

GUIDELINE

You may want to review *Exercise 3* beforehand. If there is time, students could either write the entire essay or look back at previous Task 1 essays and rewrite the introductions.

Unit 2.9 Giving and justifying opinions

You may want to start by writing an extreme (though not offensive!) opinion on the board and inviting a response from the class. Example: Children learn nothing from computer games.

GUIDELINE

2.9 EXERCISE 1 (page 45)

Students should have little difficulty in identifying that the opinion is expressed too dogmatically. You may want to elicit some possible ways of improving the dialogue before looking at the Point of Impact and *Exercise 2*.

GUIDELINE

2.9 EXERCISE 2 (page 45)

Examples:
It is my opinion …, I believe …, As I see it …, To be honest …, To be frank …, In my opinion …, I'm convinced that …, As far as I'm concerned …, From my point of view …, It seems to me that ….

SUGGESTED ANSWER

2.9 EXERCISE 3 (page 45)

GUIDELINE

Ensure that students are using the language from *Exercise 2* for this exercise.

2.9 EXERCISE 4 (page 46)

GUIDELINE

This exercise could be used as an opportunity to brainstorm ideas your class may have limited opinions about. For example:

• importance of leisure time versus commitment to company
• having freedom at a young age to travel, etc. (advantages/disadvantages)
• male/female roles and societies' expectations
• motivations for students to study overseas and availability of places
• reality versus gender stereotypes.

EXTENSION ACTIVITY

You could split the class into teams and set up a role play, getting them to give and justify opinions from contrasting perspectives. They could be politicians discussing lowering the drinking age, TV critics with different opinions about a popular film, or students talking about the IELTS exam. Remind them that they do not necessarily have to express their own opinions, so long as they justify them.

Unit 2.10   Multiple choice (listening)

2.10 EXERCISE 1 (page 46)

GUIDELINE

This is simply to get students into the idea that they are looking for defining features of each option in multiple-choice questions, e.g. what information is the same/different in the answer choices.

2.10 EXERCISE 2 (page 46)

**GUIDELINE
ANSWER**

The differences lie in the places (*gym, library, video club*). The other information does not highlight differences (*joining, becoming a member, asking about membership*).

2.10 EXERCISE 3 (page 47)

**SUGGESTED
ANSWER**

The Point of Impact draws attention to the use of parallel expressions.

1 **Is hoping to** could become *wants to, is trying to*, **6 months** could become *half a year*.
2 **As proof of identity** could become *for ID*, **student card** could be *card from my school*, **bank card** could become *cash card* or *ATM card*.
3 **Mobile** could become *cellphone*, **e-mail** could become *via computer* or *electronically*.
4 **half an hour** could become *30 minutes*, **bus/train** could become *public transport*.
5 **Weekly** could become *per week*, **cost** could become *price* or *rent*, **estate agent** could become *real estate agent* or *realtor*, **sign** could become *board*, **owner** could become *landlord*.
6 **Deposit** could become *bond* or *money paid in advance*, **equivalent** could become *the same as*.

2.10 EXERCISE 4 (page 47)

ANSWER

1	B		4	D
2	A		5	B
3	A		6	C

2.10 EXERCISE 5 (page 47)

Students may be better pooling their ideas in pairs or small groups.

GUIDELINE

2.10 EXERCISE 6 (page 48)

Students should listen first for the answer, then again to match the three other points (directly contradicted, indirectly contradicted or not exact).

ANSWER

The correct answer	Directly contradicted	Indirectly contradicted	Not exact
C	D	A	B

2.10 EXERCISE 7 (page 48)

The transformation sentences do not cover the whole statement (see the Point of Impact that follows). (A) win because of a positive mental attitude – *They feel positive*, the note doesn't say that they win. (B) *occasionally* has been ignored. (C) they don't *talk to*, they are *under considerable pressure from* the media.

ANSWER

2.10 EXERCISE 8 (page 48)

This exercise should be an opportunity for students to review all the skills of the lesson. You may choose to quickly recap before students begin.

GUIDELINE

2.10 EXERCISE 9 and REVIEW (page 49)

There is a short pause in the tape. You may want to stop the tape for one minute here as this represents a change of question style from multiple choice to short answer. In the real IELTS test, it is very common to have a break in one section of the listening, but this is not really highlighted during the course in case students do have a listening without a break.

GUIDELINE

1	D		6	cheaper
2	B		7	(having a) pension(s)
3	B		8	negative equity
4	C		9	(enormously) satisfying
5	B		10	raise (your) hand

ANSWER

Unit 2.11   Building a paragraph

This is the first of two lessons on paragraphing. The most important aim of the lesson is to get students thinking about topic sentences and how they should structure a paragraph.

2.11 EXERCISE 1 (page 49)

The focus here is on getting students to see the relationship between the topic sentence (usually the opening sentence of the paragraph) and how it affects the rest of the paragraph. By opening the topic sentence with 'Nothing ... more' and using the word 'stress' as the end focus of the sentence, it can be assumed that the paragraph continues to talk about stress in modern lifestyles.

2.11 EXERCISE 2 (page 49)

The correct topic sentence is (a). Although the words 'common(ly)' and 'workplace' are both in the paragraph, the focus is clearly the positive and the negative aspects.

2.11 EXERCISE 3 (pages 49–50)

A   Free time is increasingly vital these days.

B   There is an increasing dependence on 'junk' food.

C   E-mail is not as effective a means of communication as more traditional forms.

2.11 EXERCISE 4 (page 50)

This exercise should give students the opportunity to consolidate what they have learned. After they have organised the paragraph, you should get them to justify their order using steps from the lesson. Answers: e, b a, d, c

Before moving on to the final exercise, you could draw attention to the Point of Impact. An example of such a qualifying statement/concession can be found in sentence c of *Exercise 4*.

2.11 EXERCISE 5 (page 50)

If students are having trouble thinking of ideas, you could brainstorm as a class before they write.

Unit 2.12   Topic Card: Leisure interests

2.12 EXERCISE 1 (page 51)

The most obvious tenses are going to be the past simple/used to, but see if you can elicit a wider range of responses from students. Suggested answers are given in *Exercise 2*.

2.12 EXERCISE 2 (page 51)

a   I *used to* love going to the fairground.

b   It *was* so exciting to see all the attractions.

c   I *haven't been* to one [a fairground] since I was 12.

d Once, when I was about nine, my father wouldn't let me go on any more attractions because I *had eaten* two bags of candy floss.

2.12 EXERCISE 3 (page 51)

Refer to Unit 1.12 for suggestions on how to use the topic card.

EXTENSION ACTIVITY

You could use the following extension questions to follow the topic card from *Exercise 1*.

How important is it for children to have proper educational toys?
Do you think children's education has changed much since you were a child?
What changes do you see in children's education in the future?

The world around us

3

Unit 3.1   Parallel expressions (reading)

3.1 EXERCISE 1 (page 52)

ANSWER

The answers for the three questions all come directly from the text.
The purpose of this exercise is highlighted in the Point of Impact that follows.

A The petroleum industry.   C Car manufacturers.

B Green trees and bright blue skies.

3.1 EXERCISE 2 (page 52)

ANSWER

Question	Point of Impact number
A	3
B	1
C	2

3.1 EXERCISE 3 (page 53)

ANSWER

Noun	Person	Verb	Passive	Adjective	Adverb	Alternative vocabulary
pollution pollutant	_____	to pollute	be polluted	polluted	_____	SYNONYM contaminant, impurity, toxin, effluence ANTONYM clean
ecology	ecologist	_____	_____	ecological	ecologically	SYNONYM natural science, biology, environmental science, naturalist ANTONYM
nature	naturalist	to naturalise	be naturalised	natural	naturally	SYNONYM environment, natural world, ecology, ecologist ANTONYM
endangerment	_____	to endanger	be endangered	endangered	_____	SYNONYM imperil, jeopardise, put at risk, prolific ANTONYM
industry	industrialist	to industrialise	be industrialised	industrial	industrially	SYNONYM manufacturing, business, trade, production, developed ANTONYM
conservation	conservationist	to conserve	be conserved	conservative	conservatively	SYNONYM preservation, protection, upkeep, ANTONYM destruction
destruction	destroyer	to destroy	be destroyed	destructive	destructively	SYNONYM annihilate, devastate, demolish, ruin, damage ANTONYM build, construct

3.1 EXERCISE 4 (page 53)

The sentences in this exercise combine to create a paragraph about the environmental impact of car driving. Rather than substitute vocabulary in each sentence, you could ask stronger students to consider the whole paragraph and change the sentence structures. No model answer is given here as there are a number of alternatives.

3.1 EXERCISE 5 (page 54)

1 A deterioration in lakes and forests in northern Europe was first noticed in *probably a time.*

2 Pollution in rain is a result of *maybe a specific chemical name.*

3 Nearly half of manmade sources of acid rain are due to *could be pollution or some kind of industry.*

4 Some animals have declined in number by over 50% because of scarcer *could be connected to their food source or natural habitat.*

5 Land used for farming is becoming *something negative – weaker? less useful?*

6 Urban household water supplies are contaminated by *toxins, pollution or specific pollution type.*

7 Air pollution is travelling further as it is disgorged through *probably some way pollution is spread.*

8 Legislation passed in the 1980s and the 1990s was a response to *excess pollution? rising pollution? Pressure from the public? Political pressure?*

3.1 EXERCISE 6 (page 54)

There are many different ways students could answer this exercise, but like *Exercise 4* there are a number of words that can be transformed.

3.1 EXERCISE 7 (pages 54–55)

1	the late 1970s	5	less productive
2	acids	6	toxic metals
3	transportation	7	tall chimneys
4	food sources	8	transboundary pollution

3.1 REVIEW (page 55)

9	A	viii	13	E	i
10	B	iv	14	F	ii
11	C	x	15	G	vi
12	D	vii			

Unit 3.2   Describing approximate data

GUIDELINE

An essential skill in IELTS Writing is the ability to use a number of varied structures. Make sure you draw students' attention to the Point of Impact.

3.2 EXERCISE 1 (page 56)

ANSWER

The description has too much data presented as percentages – it is repetitive and copies almost directly from the graph.

3.2 EXERCISE 2 (page 56)

GUIDELINE

You are aiming to elicit some of the expressions used in *Exercise 3*. You may be better using *Exercise 1* as a board example and brainstorming as a class for this exercise.

3.2 EXERCISE 3 (page 56)

ANSWER

a	a tenth	g	nearly half
b	a fifth	h	half
c	a quarter	i	over half
d	slightly more than a fifth	j	three quarters
e	slightly less than a third	k	just over three quarters
f	a third	l	the vast majority/almost all

GUIDELINE

As you complete *Exercise 3*, you may find that students produce some variations to the expressions. They should add them to the list at this point, so they have a page for future reference.

ANSWER

3.2 EXERCISE 4 (page 56)

Biggest ◀——————————————————————▶ Smallest					
1 all	**2** the vast majority	**3** the majority	**4** many	**6** a minority	**8** very few
			5 a considerable number	**7** a few	**9** almost none

3.2 EXERCISE 5 (page 57)

GUIDELINE

After the example sentence, students should be writing eight more sentences using the remaining expressions.

3.2 EXERCISE 6 (page 57)

ANSWER

1 B   4 A

2 C   5 E

3 D

3.2 EXERCISE 7 (page 57)

Although tables are studied in greater detail in Unit 5.8, students should be able to write a number of sentences using the language presented in this section.

GUIDELINE

Unit 3.3   Your hometown

You could start by using a mind map to brainstorm topics related to social issues. This is quite a broad subject, covering aspects from your hometown and city life through to unemployment and crime. Students should be able to justify the connection between the topic they raise and the theme of social issues.

GUIDELINE

3.3 EXERCISE 1 (page 58)

This is explained in the Point of Impact that follows.

GUIDELINE

3.3 EXERCISE 2 (page 58)

With the added phrases, the dialogue should now read:

ANSWER

> I'm from Bahrain in the Arabian Gulf. It has a population of over 600 000 which is quite small in comparison with some of our Middle Eastern neighbours. It is quite cool in winter but very hot in summer. I much prefer the cooler weather. The main industries are banking and pearl diving, although tourism is becoming increasingly important. Oil is not so important, yet many people think it is our main source of revenue.

3.3 EXERCISE 3 (page 58)

You might want to brainstorm for some descriptive adjectives before you begin this exercise (historic, open, sprawling, well planned, etc.). Encourage students to think of things that are unique to their hometown, such as particular buildings, festivals, local crafts or products, etc. A useful exercise would be to present a well-known place, such as London, referring to London Bridge, Buckingham Palace, etc. This could serve as a model for the students.

GUIDELINE

3.3 EXERCISE 4 (page 58)

After you have checked students have some relevant points in *Exercise 3*, *Exercise 4* allows students to put the whole lesson together. You might want students to write complete sentences or notes, but be aware of the Point of Impact that follows.

GUIDELINE

3.3 EXERCISE 5 (page 59)

With students in pairs, it is often a good idea to make sure that Student A is not reading from *Exercise 4*. After Student A and B have finished, switch them round so all students have a chance to speak and take notes.

GUIDELINE

WRITING SPEAKING SPEAKING SPEAKING SPEAKING SPEAKING SPEAKING

Unit 3.4   Numbers, dates and letters (listening)

3.4 EXERCISE 1 (page 59)

ANSWER

1	c	6	i
2	g	7	j
3	h	8	e
4	f	9	b
5	a	10	d

3.4 EXERCISE 2 (page 59)

SUGGESTED ANSWER

Answers could include time, date, cost, distance, per cent, phone number, number in a list.

3.4 EXERCISE 3 (page 59)

ANSWER

a	Twelve thousand six hundred and eighteen	12 618
b	Seventeen thousand and two	17 002
c	Seventy four thousand, two hundred and seventy two	74 272
d	Eight million four hundred thousand	8 400 000
e	One million, four hundred and twenty two thousand six hundred and nineteen	1 422 619
f	Seven billion, eight hundred and eighteen million, six hundred and fourteen thousand, nine hundred and ninety three	7 818 614 993

3.4 EXERCISE 4 (page 60)

ANSWER

1	13	National parks in New Zealand.
2	27%	more men than women in Korea.
3	20	people can be killed by the King cobra's venom.
4	90%	of the universe is composed of hydrogen.
5	$1 billion	was made by the movie *Titanic*.
6	Three million	works of art are in an art gallery in St Petersburg.

3.4 EXERCISE 5 (page 60)

GUIDELINE

This exercise depends on the date, but the main idea is to show students that dates have different constructions, as shown in the Point of Impact after the exercise.

3.4 EXERCISE 6 (page 60)

This exercise is very similar to *Exercise 4*, but concentrates on different date constructions.

ANSWER

1 World War II ended on the 11th of November, 1945.

2 Princess Diana died on August 30th 1997.

3 On September 11th 2001 the Twin Towers in America were attacked.

4 England won the World Cup on the 30th of July 1966.

5 President John F. Kennedy was assassinated in November 1963, on the 22nd I think.

6 The *Titanic* sank on April the 14th, 1912.

EXTENSION ACTIVITY

A short recording of radio or TV news often has figures. In addition, you can extend this easily by getting students to give information about any event for which they have ready statistics.

Unit 3.5   Preparing a plan for Task II

Like with Task I, many students feel that the time pressure in the IELTS exam precludes any chance of preparing a plan and they end up writing a disjointed essay that does not really follow its main points through. It is important that students understand the value of planning in order to present a unified and logical argument. This has been covered partly in 'Brainstorming' (Unit 1.5).

GUIDELINE

3.5 EXERCISE 1 (page 61)

Should we work a four-day week?

ANSWER

3.5 EXERCISE 2 (page 61)

Students could also add any ideas they have to the two sides of each question.

ANSWER

a Should the government place a higher tax on private cars? Yes it should/No it shouldn't.

b Is education that does not lead to direct employment a waste? Yes it is/No it isn't.

c Are many countries ignoring the problem of global warming? Yes they are/No they are not.

d Are celebrities unfairly taking money that should go to other causes? Yes they are/No they are not.

e How much should the government enforce healthy lifestyles? Not much/A lot.

3.5 EXERCISE 3 (pages 61–62)

From the Point of Impact, point 1 is *Have advances in technology improved our lifestyle?* (Underlined words are the topic words.)

Points 2–4 may be best done as group work.

**GUIDELINE
ANSWER**

3.5 EXERCISE 4 (page 62)

GUIDELINE

This is a particularly difficult area for many students who can think of an opinion but cannot expand their ideas. It may be better to continue working as a class to brainstorm these points before students add more ideas of their own. It is also a good opportunity to check for spelling errors.

3.5 EXERCISE 5 (page 62)

GUIDELINE

This exercise depends on the ideas that have been brainstormed, but there should be at least one idea and supporting evidence in each paragraph.

3.5 EXERCISE 6 (page 62)

GUIDELINE

This essay title is similar to that of *Exercise 3*, to make it easier to apply the points from *Exercises 2, 3, 4* and *5*.

Unit 3.6   Describing places

GUIDELINE

This lesson should consolidate Unit 3.3 ('Your hometown'), as well as adding some extra vocabulary to talk about places.

3.6 EXERCISE 1 (page 63)

ANSWER

O awe-inspiring	**W** tropical	**O** peaceful	**O** amazing	**O** breathtaking
W humid	**O** serene	**O** spectacular	**C** rugged	**O** lively
O packed	**C** mountainous	**O** pleasant	**W** clear	**C** hilly
C green	**W** sun-drenched			

3.6 EXERCISE 2 (page 63)

ANSWER

Well, one place I love in New Zealand is Tongariro National Park. You can do the Tongariro circuit – you walk right around the mountains, staying in huts. It takes about three days. The views are *absolutely* ^a**spectacular** – on a ^b**clear** day you can see all the way to Mount Taranaki in the west. It can be *extremely* hot, yet as with any ^c**mountainous** environment, the temperature can drop *incredibly* quickly, so you have to be prepared. At weekends or holidays, it can get a little crowded, and some nights the huts are ^d**packed**, but everyone is so ^e**pleasant**. I must have said 'Hello' a hundred times a day when I was there!

3.6 EXERCISE 3 (page 63)

GUIDELINE

Students should already be familiar with the concept of intensifiers. As they use them in the lesson, check for the correct intonation.

3.6 EXERCISE 4 (page 63)

GUIDELINE

Students should avoid simply rehashing the work they have done on their hometown. This should be an opportunity to describe a place they like. It could be a place where they have been on holiday or simply somewhere they have heard about. It is worth reminding students once again that 'recited' responses will not get a good result, so once they have written their paragraph and you have checked it, they should avoid simply reading their work.

EXTENSION ACTIVITY

Write a short paragraph about two different places. One should be a positive description and one should be negative, pointing out the less attractive aspects.

Unit 3.7 Short-answer questions (reading)

This section should give students practice in applying the parallel expressions they studied in Unit 3.1.

GUIDELINE

3.7 EXERCISE 1 (page 64)

b is better. Short-answer questions ask for a maximum number of words (normally three or less). Students should be familiar with this instruction by now.

ANSWER

3.7 EXERCISE 2 (page 64)

a Who / earthquakes / movement / tectonic plates
b How many / types / shock wave
c Which / shock waves / stronger
d What / tectonic plates / sit on
e What kind / earthquake / subterranean experiments
f What / main danger / earthquakes / urban areas
g What / interpreted / warning sign / earthquakes
h Where / earthquake prediction / successful.

ANSWER

3.7 EXERCISE 3 (page 64)

a found / discovered / determined / caused by / because of / shifts
b number / sorts
c more powerful / more intense
d rest on / lie on / above / on top of
e underground / testing
f biggest problem / major threat / built up / houses / buildings
g seen as / herald / portent
h accurate / helpful / estimate

SUGGESTED ANSWER

3.7 EXERCISE 4 (page 65)

a	Robert Mallet	d	molten lava	g	foreshocks
b	two	e	artificial	h	Haicheng
c	primary	f	falling objects		

ANSWER

3.7 REVIEW (pages 66–67)

This reviews the question styles from Unit 2.3, Unit 3.3 and this section.

ANSWER

1 v	8 America/the USA
2 i	9 corrosion
3 vii	10 engineers
4 viii	11 expensive/the cost
5 hot rocks/aquifers	12 hotter temperatures
6 fossil fuels	13 naturally thermal
7 the Romans	14 radon

EXTENSION ACTIVITY

You could get students asking each other general knowledge questions that require short answers. You could ask students to prepare a short reading text first if there is sufficient time.

Unit 3.8 Comparing and contrasting data

GUIDELINE

In this section, you are looking at comparing and contrasting data. In Unit 4.5, you will cover comparison and contrast in Task II. Although many of the structures are the same, the application is a little different. This lesson should also consolidate Unit 3.1 in which students looked at describing approximate data.

3.8 EXERCISE 1 (page 67)

ANSWER

America has the highest level of pollution, New Zealand the lowest.

3.8 EXERCISE 2 (page 67)

SUGGESTED ANSWER

Task I can ask you to compare a number of variables, but perhaps the most common are: years, places, people (gender, race, age, education, etc.).

ANSWER

3.8 EXERCISE 3 (page 67)

	example adjective	comparative	superlative
Words with one syllable	high	higher	the highest
Words with three syllables or more	productive	more productive	the most productive
Words ending in -y	wealthy	wealthier	the wealthiest
Short words ending with a consonant/vowel/consonant	hot	hotter	the hottest
Irregular	good	better	the best

3.8 EXERCISE 4 (page 68)

This should not be too challenging for most students, but try and elicit some academic adjectives they could use before they begin.

GUIDELINE

3.8 EXERCISE 5 (page 68)

ANSWER

a Developed countries are <u>more</u> reliant on alternative energy sources <u>than</u> developing countries are.

b Solar power accounts for <u>far less</u> of the total energy production <u>than</u> gas or coal does.

c <u>The more</u> fossil fuels are used, <u>the higher</u> the level of urban pollution.

d Hydro power <u>is not as</u> efficient as wind power.

e <u>Like</u> Japan, South Korea does not produce any natural gas.

3.8 EXERCISE 6 (page 68)

Much like with *Exercise 4*, make sure students use academic sentences.

GUIDELINE

3.8 EXERCISE 7 (page 68)

Review becomes increasingly important as the course builds, so you should spend a considerable amount of time making sure students have remembered and are applying what they have learned.

GUIDELINE

Unit 3.9 Misunderstandings

3.9 EXERCISE 1 (page 69)

The best answer is given by Candidate 2, as explained in the Point of Impact that follows.

ANSWER

3.9 EXERCISE 2 (page 69)

Students will look at the third category ('a question you have never thought about') in Unit 5.9.

ANSWER

1 E	2 A	3 B	4 C	5 D

3.9 EXERCISE 3 (page 69)

Students may need some ideas before they can begin, but they should be recycling the phrases presented in *Exercise 2*. If not, you could take the role of the examiner and set the situations in which the language has to be used.

GUIDELINE

EXTENSION ACTIVITY

Pairs of students could create a dialogue in which all the phrases from *Exercise 2* are used.

Unit 3.10   Table completion (listening)

3.10 EXERCISE 1 (page 69)

SUGGESTED ANSWER

There are no exact answers for this exercise, but students should be able to predict the following:

1 is probably a European city
2 is an expensive but fast form of transport, probably plane.
3 is a date which must be in the northern hemisphere's summer months.
4 is a price. Being a coach trip, it's likely to be the cheapest. It is also in UK sterling.

The Point of Impact explains that although this exercise is a little easier than students could expect, it highlights the important skills.

3.10 EXERCISE 2 (page 70)

GUIDELINE

This builds on *Exercise 1* and the Point of Impact. Students should be able to predict some information, but you should draw students' attention to the line in the box regarding Sam's comments on 'Ideas for the future'. This indicates that no information is given. Students should not expect to fill every cell in every table.

3.10 EXERCISE 3 (page 70)

As there is no word limit for this exercise, the exact way students phrase their answers is not as important as getting the main ideas. Below are some suggestions.

SUGGESTED ANSWER

1 Thinks it can be difficult
2 Always recycles
3 Limited local facilities

4 Very limited facilities
5 Fine offenders

3.10 EXERCISE 4 (page 70)

SUGGESTED ANSWER

After reading the Point of Impact, students should use this exercise to review all the skills so far, especially logic and word families. There is no listening, but they should be able to predict the following table.

	indicators	frequency	response
earthquake	vibrations, tremors	common	find shelter in doorways or open ground
volcano	heat, escaping gas, rising water temperatures	rare	evacuate the area, find high ground
tsunami	**noun(s), something connected with water or the sea**	**(frequency adjective)**	**verb of action, something about moving from coastal areas**
tornado	**Noun(s) connected with wind**	**(frequency adjective)**	close and lock all windows, stay inside
avalanche	**Noun(s) often connected with snow**	occasional	**verb of action, something about moving away from overhanging areas**
forest fires	rising air temperature, unusual animal and bird activity	**(frequency adjective)**	**verb of action, maybe cutting, clearing, soaking. Also possibly evacuation**

3.10 REVIEW (page 71)

1	1 hour	**6**	hunters
2	conservation issues	**7**	6000
3	the USA	**8**	agriculture
4	(prides of) lions	**9**	B
5	50 000	**10**	C

Unit 3.11 Giving and justifying opinions

3.11 EXERCISE 1 (page 72)

It is too direct, and presents itself as fact rather than opinion without concessions or justification. The Point of Impact that follows is in part a review of previous units.

ANSWER

3.11 EXERCISE 2 (page 72)

Some possible options:

It has been said …   It seems that …

Many people hold …

SUGGESTED ANSWER

3.11 EXERCISE 3 (page 72)

Remind students that they can use negative constructions (e.g. Some people believe that extinction is not simply a natural process of evolution). The following are only possible answers.

1 It is generally accepted that extinction is a natural process of evolution.
2 Many people believe that better control of deforestation could be achieved through international pressure.
3 It could be argued that it is immoral to keep animals in captivity.
4 It seems that more support from the government would make ecotourism more popular.

SUGGESTED ANSWER

3.11 EXERCISE 4 (page 72)

This depends on what students have answered for *Exercise 3*.

GUIDELINE

3.11 EXERCISE 5 (page 72)

ANSWER

It could be argued that green issues have been excessively debated. **While I admit that** concern for the environment is very important, a less intense approach to problems may have better results.

The linking phrase is one of concession.

WRITING

3.11 EXERCISES 6, 7 & 8 (page 73)

GUIDELINE

There are a number of possible answers. It may be better to work as a group wherever possible. Students should use a variety of concession words so may need to review Unit 1.2 before beginning.

3.11 EXERCISE 9 (page 73)

GUIDELINE

This should be a review of this part of the unit. You may decide to brainstorm as a class or even plan the essay before students begin writing.

SPEAKING

Unit 3.12   Topic Card: The world around us

As with the other topics, there are a number of ways in which this lesson can be used.

3.12 EXERCISE 1 (page 74)

GUIDELINE

As is explained throughout the course, adjectives are very important in the speaking test. This exercise should be used as a practical example of using adjectives to describe place (Unit 3.6).

3.12 EXERCISES 2 & 3 (page 74)

GUIDELINE

Students should be familiar with this approach by now.

EXTENSION ACTIVITY

Do you think tourism has had a negative effect on some cultures?

What is the importance of travel?

Do you think that young people today have more opportunities than previous generations had?

UNIT 4
Cultural concerns

Unit 4.1 Qualifying words (reading)

In this lesson, students will be answering some TRUE or FALSE questions. The skills for this particular question type, as well as NOT GIVEN, will be studied in detail in Unit 4.7.

4.1 EXERCISE 1 (page 75)

All the statements are false, as explained in the Point of Impact that follows.

ANSWER

4.1 EXERCISE 2 (pages 75–76)

A = 3	D = 2
B = 4	E = 1
C = 6	F = 5

ANSWER

4.1 EXERCISE 3 (page 76)

Virtual culture

A Culture is defined as the 'socially transmitted behaviour patterns, arts, beliefs, and institutions that are the expression of a particular class, community or period' (www.dictionary.com). To <u>most</u> people, this is seen in terms of books, paintings, rituals and ceremonies, but recently there has been a new entrant in the field of what is considered to be 'culture' – the Internet.

B   On the Internet, science and art, media and mind combine to create a modern culture which is far more widespread than any of its predecessors. Not referring to the casual user who has no particular interest in the Internet, active supporters of the Internet as a culture have given themselves nomenclature to reflect their cultural aspirations – they are the new cyberpoets. A cyberpoet can be defined as 'one who makes frequent trips to the edge of technology, society and traditional culture and strives to be artful in their use of virtual space'.

C   Supporter or opponent of this new culture, there is <u>little doubt</u> that the Internet offers <u>a lot</u> to our traditional view of culture. In just <u>a few</u> minutes in front of a keyboard, we can read <u>almost</u> anything that has ever been written, yet no paper had to be made, no library had to stay open and thus the cost remains minimal. <u>All</u> of this encourages even the casual surfer to explore further than he or she otherwise would have. The same effect can be observed with works of art. Previously available to be viewed only in museums if they were not in the hands of private collectors, <u>all but a few</u> famous works are now replicated on the Internet.

D   Yet the Internet is not merely a mirror of traditional culture – it is also a new culture in its own right. The medium of the Net allows for wider distribution and new platforms for <u>most</u> forms of art. 'Kinetic art' and other such computerised art forms occur with increasing regularity, both motivated by and generating an upsurge in popular and computer-mediated art.

E   In addition, if culture is said to be 'socially transmitted', then the Internet is remarkable in its ability to share, on <u>an almost global scale,</u> all the factors that constitute culture. We have only to hear the influence of jargon as we visit dub-dub-dub dot sites and surf the web to see how international the Internet has become <u>to the majority</u>.

F   <u>Very few people</u> would disagree that the cyberpoets are increasingly asserting themselves into popular culture. What is not so certain is how far this will go, as the Internet continues to assimilate more and more forms of culture, reaching global audiences. It is not inconceivable that our <u>entire</u> perception of culture will soon become cyber-focused.

4.1 EXERCISE 4 (page 77)

ANSWER

a	T	c	F	e	T
b	F	d	F	f	F

4.1 REVIEW (page 77)

GUIDELINE

These exercises are different from previous units in that it is the responsibility of the students to come up with the questions. Group work or pair work may be more effective than working alone, but that depends on your particular class. If students are working in pairs, one student should look at a different reading.

Unit 4.2   Describing data with prepositions

4.2 EXERCISE 1 (page 77)

GUIDELINE

Students should be able to complete these sentences without much help. The axes of the graph are not defined as the exercise concentrates on *how* to describe rather than *what* to describe.

ANSWER

a	It started at 2	e	It decreased from 10 to 4
b	There was an increase of 8	f	There was a drop of 6
c	It increased by 8	g	It fluctuated at around 4
d	It peaked at 10	h	It finished at 5

4.2 EXERCISE 2 (pages 77–78)

GUIDELINE

This exercise uses the prepositions in a paragraph format. If students seem confident, you may want to draw a graph on the board and get them to create the whole paragraph themselves.

ANSWER

a	from	d	at	g	to
b	to	e	to		
c	of	f	by		

4.2 EXERCISE 3 (page 79)

Before moving on to *Exercise 4*, where students consider the use of prepositions further, use *Exercise 3* to check their understanding of what the data in the table actually means.

ANSWER

a at 3% – refers to 5–15-year-old females using the Internet.

b ranged between 23% and 80% – the lowest and highest % of females (by age group) using the fiction section.

c from 71% to 22% – the fall of males using the fiction section between 5–15 and 16–25.

d from 9% at – males using the non-fiction section aged 16–25.

e within a 2% range – the result for males and females aged 66 and above using the fiction section.

f between the ages of 26 and 65 – refers to a statistic somewhere in the third age category.

4.2 EXERCISE 4 (page 79)

ANSWER

1	b	4	d
2	a	5	e
3	c	6	f

4.2 EXERCISE 5 (page 79)

Before students begin this exercise, ensure that they have a title for the graph and a scale for the axes.

GUIDELINE

4.2 EXERCISE 6 (page 79)

This should include a plan as well as suitable prepositions.

GUIDELINE

Unit 4.3 Festivals

4.3 EXERCISE 1 (pages 79–80)

A Christmas Day

B Bonfire Night (this may be difficult for many students)

C Valentine's Day

ANSWER

4.3 EXERCISE 2 (page 80)

In the second column (Why is it special?) they should be writing some specifics about the event. For example:

GUIDELINE

SUGGESTED ANSWER

Special occasion/event	Why is it special?
Christmas Day	lights, tree, presents, crackers, cheerful people
	Origin: celebrates the birth of Jesus

4.3   EXERCISE 3 (page 80)

GUIDELINE

If possible, get students in your class making notes about different events so they are not reporting about the same events or occasions.

4.3   EXERCISE 4 (page 80)

GUIDELINE

As with any speaking practice, quietly monitor students noting common errors for correction later.

Unit 4.4   Listening for details

GUIDELINE

A large part of this lesson does not really involve the students' book. Before you begin any of the exercises, you could elicit what students think is meant by 'Listening for details'. It is largely a review of earlier units of the book: personal information, numbers, dates, letters, spelling. Here students should be focusing on the specifics of what they hear. The following exercises practise the main points involved in listening for details.

4.4   EXERCISE 1 (page 80)

ANSWER

a   1946 – UNESCO formed
b   180 – nations in UNESCO
c   60 – worldwide offices
d   2001 – General Conference

4.4   EXERCISE 2 (page 80)

Any date construction is acceptable.

ANSWER

a   Bastille Day – 14 July
b   Elvis's death – 16 August
c   Burns' Night – 25 January
d   Martin Luther King Day – 4 April
e   ANZAC Day – 25 April

4.4   EXERCISE 3 (page 81)

ANSWER

a   (Adrian) Wolffe
b   Llangollen
c   Navajo Indians
d   Athapaksan

4.4   EXERCISE 4 (page 81)

ANSWER

a   Some people do not fully appreciate cultural heritage.
b   Many young people see the value in traditions.
c   Most traditional cultures will almost certainly not disappear.

4.5   EXERCISE 5 (page 81)

GUIDELINE

Students should be noting as many specific details as they can. You may need to replay the recording more than once.

EXTENSION ACTIVITY

Students prepare a report of their own, and read it to their partner or the class. This is an opportunity for students to practise writing as well as listening. Remind students to include specific details, such as dates, numbers, etc., in keeping with the lesson focus.

Unit 4.5 Comparison and contrast in Task II

4.5 EXERCISE 1 (page 81)

This exercise is intended only to get students considering what aspects can be compared/contrasted. Some examples:

SUGGESTED ANSWER

a   architecture, age, history, business
b   length, popularity, age group
c   longevity, availability to general public.

4.5 EXERCISE 2 (pages 81–82)

ANSWER

a TRUE	e TRUE
b FALSE	f TRUE
c TRUE	g TRUE
d FALSE	h FALSE

4.5 EXERCISE 3 (page 82)

ANSWER

Compare	Contrast
likewise	while
equally	as opposed to
in the same way	however
in a similar way	in contrast to
as well as	whereas
Like the Louvre …	by contrast
as … as …	although
similarly	instead of

4.5 EXERCISE 4 (page 82)

Ensure that students are using different points to compare and contrast for each sentence, not simply rewording each one with different comparing/contrasting vocabulary. You might find it easier to brainstorm as a class first.

GUIDELINE

ANSWER   **4.5**   EXERCISE **5** (page 82)

Verbs:	Adjectives:	Nouns:
EXAMPLE		
compare (with/to)	compared (with/to)	in comparison with
contrast (with)	contrasting	contrast/in contrast to
differ (from)/differentiate (between)	different (from)	difference (between)
distinguish (between)	distinct (from)/as distinct from	distinction (between)
resemble	the same as/similar (to)	resemblance (to/with)/similarity (with)
vary (from/between)	variation (between)	

GUIDELINE   After students have completed the table, you could get them to refer back to *Exercise 4* and think of other sentences using some of the vocabulary from this exercise.

4.5   REVIEW   (page 83)

GUIDELINE   Be aware that this may be the first time students have seen the task word 'Discuss'.

Unit 4.6   Comparing and contrasting

4.6   EXERCISE **1** (page 83)

GUIDELINE   Many students may simply answer 'English', but get them to consider areas of difficulty that a learner would face when learning their language. For example, many Asian languages present the difficulty of using different alphabets.

The main focus of Unit 4 is culture and *Exercises 2, 3* and *4* focus on traditional food. However, Unit 6.3 focuses on 'food' as it relates to health. Although this is not a problem as they approach this subject from different angles, there are some discussions you may want to delay until the later unit.

4.6   EXERCISE **2** (page 83)

ANSWER   Comparing and contrasting allow students to relate the food they are discussing to something which may be more familiar with the examiner.

4.6   EXERCISE **3** (page 83)

GUIDELINE   The third column needs a country. India, for example, could elicit such comparisons as 'equally spicy'. Some of the vocabulary and structures you use here will be from the Writing course, but what you are aiming at here is some of the more common spoken forms of comparing and contrasting. You may want to elicit more examples before getting students to talk about the notes they have made.

4.6   EXERCISE **4** (page 84)

GUIDELINE   Remember that you are focusing on the cultural aspect, and using the third prompt to elicit comparisons and contrasts.

EXTENSION ACTIVITY

Exercise 4 leads on to a possible extension activity, in which students could compare and contrast their hometowns. For example:

Student A: My hometown has some beautiful architecture.

Student B: My hometown is pretty similar. There are some striking buildings, some of which are over 500 years old.

Unit 4.7 TRUE/FALSE/NOT GIVEN-style questions

4.7 EXERCISE 1 (page 84)

Question 1 – YES
Question 2 – NOT GIVEN

ANSWER

4.7 EXERCISE 2 (page 84)

It is important for students to register two points in this exercise, both of which should be fairly obvious.

1 Question 1 talks about the views of the writer, Question 2 asks about the information given.

2 They have to write YES, NO or DOES NOT SAY for the first, and TRUE, FALSE or NOT GIVEN for the second.

ANSWER

There is not much guidance you can give students regarding the difference between the two forms. It does not always follow that one asks about fact and the other opinion, neither does it follow that YES, NO or DOES NOT SAY questions are about the writer and TRUE, FALSE or NOT GIVEN about information. For the test, the best advice is only what is given in the following Point of Impact.

GUIDELINE

4.7 EXERCISE 3 (page 85)

After reading the Point of Impact, students should be able to give you some specific skills they could apply to the questions. Bring to their attention the key skills of parallel expressions, working out word families, scanning, and identifying fact and opinion.

4.7 EXERCISE 4 (pages 85–86)

ANSWER

1 NO
2 NOT GIVEN
3 NOT GIVEN
4 YES
5 NOT GIVEN
6 NO
7 YES

4.7 REVIEW (pages 86–87)

ANSWER

8 belief
9 former
10 rational
11 ascendancy
12 religion
13 ideology
14 human sacrifice/human blood
15 Age of Enlightenment
16 religion and science
17 fully independent systems
18 natural evolution

Unit 4.8 Line graphs

GUIDELINE

This section is intended to review skills applicable to line graphs, let students look through some sample answers and then build an essay of their own which they could use as a reference guide for the future. Although students look in depth at the Task I in *Exercise 2*, you have the choice as to whether they actually write their own version. In later sections, this format will be repeated so students can build Task I essay model answers for tables (Unit 5.8), bar charts and pie charts (Unit 6.8), and processes (Unit 7.8).

4.8 EXERCISE 1 (page 88)

This is not a firm guide, but if students have a different opinion they should justify it.

SUGGESTED ANSWER

Describing trends	✔	Topic and task words	✔
Register	✔	Writing an introduction	✔
Sequencing and linking	✔	Building a paragraph	✔
Brainstorming	✗	Describing data approximately	✔
Reading the axes	✔	Comparing and contrasting data	✔
Academic writing	✔	Giving and justifying opinions	✗
Preparing a plan	✔	Describing data with prepositions	✔

4.8 EXERCISE 2 (page 88)

SUGGESTED ANSWER

You should be able to elicit a number of varied sentences, but if students need prompting, you could suggest the following.

There was an upward trend throughout the period for the total population in New Zealand.

There was a sharp increase in the number of European people in 1997.

4.8 EXERCISE 3 (page 88)

ANSWER

1	Topic words?	Population / changes / ethnic groups / New Zealand
2	Tense?	1990–2002/ past tense
3	Axes?	People / (in 1000s) / years (two-year periods)
4	About?	The changes in the proportions of ethnic groups in the population of New Zealand.
5	Trend(s)?	The number of Europeans remained relatively stable, reaching a peak in the mid-1990s. The number of Maori and Pacific Island peoples remained relatively stable. A steady increase in the total population of New Zealand. Number of Asians increased dramatically.

4.8 EXERCISE 4 (page 88)

GUIDELINE

You could use this as an opportunity to test what students have learned so far or use the samples in *Exercise 5* first for a weaker class.

4.8 EXERCISE 5 (pages 88–89)

It is essential that students realise these are typical students' essays, and not perfect models. The intention throughout this lesson is for students themselves to create at least the plan for a model essay.

GUIDELINE

ANSWER

Essay A	Essay B
Comment 1	Comment 2

EXTENSION ACTIVITY

Students could correct the sample essay errors.

Unit 4.9   Expanding your topic

4.9 EXERCISE 1 (page 90)

To expand the answers, students should be considering specific traditions with which they are familiar. In addition, they should make sure they *justify* the opinions they present.

GUIDELINE

4.9 EXERCISE 2 (page 90)

a '…they give us a sense of connection with the past.'

b '…because it can bring people together and remind us of the history we share.'

c '…traditions should also be flexible.'

d To 'continue to have relevance today'.

ANSWER

4.9 EXERCISE 3 (page 90)

This question should give students the opportunity to use the four-point checklist. For example:

SUGGESTED ANSWER

Does tourism have a negative effect on a country's culture? Yes.
Why? Visitors do not always understand/respect the host country's culture.
So? The culture begins to decline.
But? The culture of a country is sometimes the reason tourists visit.
Then? It can make the culture stronger.

Unit 4.10   Diagrams and objects (listening)

The subject of this unit is cultural concerns. One way you could introduce *Exercises 1* and *2* is with a brief discussion on the rise of the café culture.

GUIDELINE

4.10 EXERCISE 1 (page 91)

A combination of the illustration and the labels should tell students it's a professional coffee maker. If students are struggling for some reason, make sure they have read all the labels closely.

ANSWER

WRITING WRITING SPEAKING SPEAKING SPEAKING SPEAKING READING & LISTENING

4.10 EXERCISE 2 (page 91)

ANSWER

1 water level light
2 boiler meter
3 steam tap
4 drainage pipe

4.10 EXERCISE 3 (page 91)

The purpose of this exercise is not for students to learn the vocabulary needed to describe musical instruments, but to get them considering the importance of getting a clear idea of what they are looking at and to predict how labels could be described.

Possible answers

SUGGESTED ANSWER

1 Bottom of the violin, right-hand side, black, oval
2 Middle, centre, raised, up, string
3 Neck, top, thin, hold, hand
4 Cut out, waist, narrower, semi-circle
5 Body, wide, smooth, solid, wood

4.10 EXERCISE 4 (page 92)

GUIDELINE

It may be difficult to get students thinking of illustrations that still fit the subject of the unit. Once students have completed their drawings, they should then describe it to their partner, who should attempt to draw it by description. This should get students thinking in terms of shape, features and place (particularly using prepositions – *above, beside, under*, etc.).

4.10 EXERCISE 5 (page 92)

ANSWER

1 Product
2 Propellant
3 Nozzle
4 Inlet
5 Spring

EXTENSION ACTIVITY

With one student with his or her back to the board, you could draw a picture which other students have to describe. The student with his or her back to the board should attempt to recreate the picture from what other students tell him or her.

Unit 4.11 Writing an introduction to Task II

GUIDELINE

Although it may seem a little unusual to study introductions midway through the book, it is important that students have first studied how to understand the question and prepare a plan.

4.11 EXERCISE 1 (page 92)

GUIDELINE

This is a review of Task I-related lessons students have already studied. If students are having difficulty, you may want to refer back to other units.

4.11 EXERCISE **2** (page 92)

Students should be able to identify the superior introduction (Introduction A). It is superior because:

- it gives a general statement about the topic in the first sentence
- it uses as few words from the topic as possible
- it introduces a contrast to the statement in the second sentence
- it gives an indication of what the writer will talk about.

All of these reasons are addressed in *Exercise 3*.

ANSWER

4.11 EXERCISE **3** (page 93)

ANSWER

You should …		Good idea	Bad idea
a	… give a general statement about the topic in the first sentence.	✔	
b	… use as many words from the topic as possible.		✔
c	… typically introduce a contrast to the statement in the second or third sentence.	✔	
d	… rephrase the question using your own words as much as possible.	✔	
e	… write at least 70 words.		✔
f	… give a brief history to introduce the topic.		✔
g	… give an indication of what you are going to write about.	✔	

4.11 EXERCISE **4** (page 93)

The use of linking words (however, therefore, etc.) will help students match the pairs.

ANSWER

	First sentence	Second sentence
Introduction 1 (example)	5	8
Introduction 2	4	2
Introduction 3	1	7
Introduction 4	3	6

4.11 EXERCISE **5** (page 94)

This is similar to the vocabulary sheets found in the reading and listening book.

ANSWER

Verb	Noun	Adjective	Adverb
a to cultivate	a culture	b cultural	culturally
c to solve	a solution		
to improve	d an improvement	e improved/improving	
f to benefit	g a benefit	beneficial	

4.11 EXERCISE **6** (page 94)

The main focus of this exercise is combining both the rephrasing and the contrasting idea of an introduction. There are a number of different ways this can be done, but remember that not every word needs to be rephrased.

GUIDELINE

4.11 EXERCISE 7 (page 94)

GUIDELINE

The difference between this introduction and that in *Exercise 1* is explained in the Point of Impact that follows. As to whether it is better or not depends on personal choice.

4.11 EXERCISE 8 (page 94)

This exercise reviews this section and former units of the book, especially Unit 3.2, which suggested that planning helps you write an introduction.

EXTENSION ACTIVITY

Students could write an introduction for the following essay title.

The quality of a society is defined by its interest in the arts. Discuss.

Unit 4.12   Topic Card: Culture

GUIDELINE

Refer to Teacher's notes Unit 1.12 for suggestions on using the topic card.
You may want to brainstorm some well-known festivals (e.g. Christmas) in preparation for *Exercise 1*.

4.12 EXERCISE 1 (page 95)

ANSWER

The final prompt on the card asks students to compare and contrast and should be a review of Unit 4.6.

4.12 EXERCISE 2 (page 95)

GUIDELINE

You may want to get students writing their answers first to ensure that they have a varied number of comparisons and contrasts.

Unit 5.1 Reading for meaning

5.1 EXERCISE 1 (page 96)

'Has nothing like' introduces the subject of indirect sentences (students should also apply simple logic to understand the question). The correct answer is C.

ANSWER

5.1 EXERCISE 2 (pages 96–97)

1	C	4	C	7	A
2	B	5	A	8	A
3	C	6	B		

ANSWER

5.1 EXERCISE 3 (page 97)

Before this activity you could get students to look at *Exercise 2* again and find the prefixes which change the meaning of a sentence (*unlikely* and *misconception*). This is an introduction to *Exercise 4*, in which students are expected to explain the meaning of a prefix and write their own example sentence.

ANSWER

mis-	badly or incorrectly
anti-	opposite, opposed to, against
pre-	before
post-	after
ex-	a state which is no longer true or the case; formerly

5.1 EXERCISE 4 (page 97)

You may find it easier to write the prefix on the board and elicit words that are commonly associated with it. This should help students (a) identify the meaning and (b) think of an example sentence. The suggested answers here do not have example sentences, only the prefixed word.

ANSWER
SUGGESTED
ANSWER

a	inter-	between/among	interdepartmental
b	micro-	too small too see with the naked eye	microwave
c	pseudo-	false, not true, a pretence	pseudo-science
d	psycho-	connected to the mind	psychological
e	quasi-	partly, in part	quasi-success
f	eco-	connected with the environment	ecological
g	narco-	connected with numbness/stupor	narcotic

5.1 EXERCISE 5 (page 98)

ANSWER

a NO
b NO
c YES
d NO

e YES
f NOT GIVEN
g NO

5.1 REVIEW (pages 99–100)

ANSWER

1 mentors
2 long hours
3 short-term
4 NO
5 NO

6 DOES NOT SAY
7 NO
8 1998
9 elections
10 Auckland

EXTENSION ACTIVITY

One possible extension activity could be to get students to write five relatively simple sentences, then rearrange them to become more varied. As a team exercise, you could deduct a point from the team that fails to think of a new construction within a certain time limit. This is an opportunity to review not only this lesson but also previous units.

Another possible extension activity would be to briefly review suffixes in much the same way as you looked at prefixes in *Exercises 3* and *4*.

Suffix	Part of speech	Example word	Example sentence
-tion/-sion	noun	industrialisation	Rapid industrialisation has had a major environmental impact.
-ful	adjective	peaceful	The South Island is very peaceful.
-ment	noun	punishment	The punishment should fit the crime.
-less	adjective	careless	A lot of accidents are caused by careless drivers.
-ive	adjective	impressive	The modern Olympic Games are very impressive.
-ure	noun	closure	The poor state of the economy means that many new businesses are threatened with closure.
-ity	noun	possibility	There is a possibility it will rain tomorrow.
-ness	noun	openness	The government policy of openness has been well received.

Unit 5.2   Describing illustrations

This section covers a rare IELTS question type – describing illustrations. It is unusual for Task I in that it asks candidates not only to describe but also to give opinions.

5.2 EXERCISE 1 (page 100)

GUIDELINE

Students should consider both the labelled and the unlabelled parts of the building in their descriptions. This is an example of point 1 (describe an illustration) in the Point of Impact that follows.

5.2 EXERCISE 2 (page 101)

GUIDELINE

With two illustrations, students should be giving some comparative structures. If necessary, you could review Unit 4.5 before beginning this exercise. This is an example of number 2 in the Point of Impact (comparing illustrations).

5.2 EXERCISE 3 (page 101)

The sketch the students produce should look similar to the one given below.

ANSWER

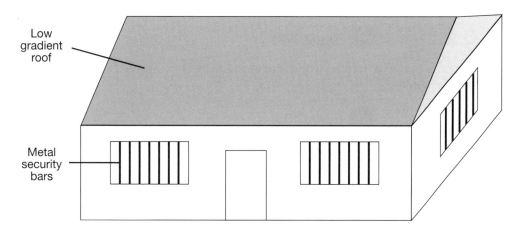

Low gradient roof

Metal security bars

5.2 EXERCISE 4 (page 102)

Extending an answer into 150 words can be a difficult task for students. Encourage them to compare/contrast and make concessions.

SUGGESTED ANSWER

Comparisons

On plan A there is a lake – good for patients to walk around, peaceful, etc. In plan B there is a mountainous area equally good as a view, but not so good to walk around.

Contrast

There is a train station on plan A whereas on B there is only the road.

Concession

In plan A the carpark is convenient to the road although it might be too noisy for patients.

EXTENSION ACTIVITY

You could get students to write the essay in class, as timed practice under exam conditions is invaluable. Alternatively, you could get students to describe a picture to another student, who should attempt to sketch it.

Unit 5.3 Food

5.3 EXERCISE 1 (page 102)

SUGGESTED ANSWER

What is your favourite food?

When do you eat it?

Where can you buy it ? / Where can you buy the ingredients?

Why do you like it?

How do you cook it? / Is it cooked?

5.3 EXERCISE 2 (page 103)

GUIDELINE

The response will vary from student to student, but encourage full answers, not just single words.

5.3 EXERCISE 3 (page 103)

SUGGESTED ANSWER

These are just some examples:

a   delicious, lovely   c   dry, bland

b   tasty, filling   d   disgusting, revolting

5.3 EXERCISE 4 (page 103)

SUGGESTED ANSWER

This is just an example of the first point (healthiness). Remember that health is the focus of this unit and will lead into *Exercise 5*.

Chinese food is better than western food because it is cooked in less fat and easier to prepare. A stir-fry meal, for example, is very healthy and can be made in minutes.

5.3 EXERCISE 5 (page 103)

SUGGESTED ANSWER

Why do you think people are eating more junk food these days?

Do you think modern technology has influenced the way we eat?

Why do you think dieting has become so popular in recent years?

EXTENSION ACTIVITY

Students ask and answer the questions from *Exercise 5*.

Unit 5.4 Note taking (listening)

5.4 EXERCISE 1 (page 103)

ANSWER

As an educated guess, the fact that the project leader complained suggests that the answer to Question 3 is 'no'. The fact that someone is a millionaire suggests that there are sufficient funds to start the investigation again. 'Not entire waste' suggests that some of the work was useful.

5.4 EXERCISE 2 (page 104)

The first time students hear the recording, they should be thinking of aspects covered in 'Listening for details' (Unit 4.4) – numbers, letters, dates, spelling, qualifying words. You may want to review this first.

GUIDELINE

5.4 EXERCISE 3 (page 104)

Students should compare their notes. This is an opportunity for you to see if they need to listen to the tape again before moving on to *Exercise 5*. This is a challenging activity. For a weaker class, introduce the questions first and conduct as a usual listening exercise.

GUIDELINE

5.4 EXERCISE 4 (page 104)

a Repetitive Strain Injury
b the computer
c (any two of the following) tightness, discomfort, stiffness, soreness, burning, coldness, numbness, pain
d take regular breaks
e light grey
f pen and paper

ANSWER

5.4 EXERCISE 5 (pages 104–105)

1 C	6 44
2 Soya (bean)	7 Cereals
3 Overcook them	8 dairy
4 They are unhealthy	9 white meat
5 21	10 Red meat

ANSWER

Unit 5.5 Improving paragraphs

This is the second lesson that looks at paragraphs (see also Unit 2.11).

GUIDELINE

5.5 EXERCISE 1 (page 105)

This is more a review of previous units. Students should notice that:

ANSWER

- the register is too informal
- the punctuation is wrong in places
- the sentences are too short (no attempt to create relative clauses, for example)
- there is no topic sentence
- it uses only the most basic linking words ('And').

'No, I don't agree', 'exercising' and 'It's more important to watch what you eat and drink, and get enough sleep' suggest that the question was probably something like *Exercise is the key to a healthy life. Do you agree?*

SUGGESTED ANSWER

READING & LISTENING

WRITING

5.5 EXERCISE 2 (page 105)

See *Exercise 3* for the improved sentences.

ANSWER

1 Poor register.
2 Could have used a linking word.
3 Could have used a relative clause.
4 The punctuation is wrong.

5.5 EXERCISE 3 (page 105)

ANSWER

1 Many people think smoking among teenagers is declining.
2 Despite legislation aimed at controlling industrial pollution, the problem still continues.
3 Exercise videos, which allow people to keep fit at home, are becoming more popular.
4 Most people prefer to drive rather than walk, even if it is only to their local shops.

5.5 EXERCISE 4 (page 106)

ANSWER

You might feel that students don't need to review linking words. However, they are a very important part of academic writing.

Listing different points	the first feature, second, finally, to conclude
For additional ideas	another, in addition, related to, furthermore, moreover, not only … but (also) …
For giving examples	for example, for instance, such as, a good example of this is
For opposite examples	but, yet, however, on the other hand, nevertheless
For stress and emphasis	in fact, what is more, in particular, notably, indeed, of course
Cause and effect	therefore, thus, as a result of, consequently, because, for this reason, if so
Time	when, while, during, subsequently, before, after
Concession	although, admittedly, even though, nonetheless

5.5 EXERCISE 5 (page 106)

ANSWER

<u>When</u> we think of lifestyles 100 years ago, we often think in terms of relative hardship, poverty and squalor. <u>However</u>, despite relatively primitive sanitation and concepts of hygiene, harmful pollution on the scale we experience today was unknown. <u>Furthermore</u>, there was a lack of awareness of long-term health effects and therefore there was little of the stress we worry about almost continually in the modern era. <u>Admittedly</u>, our life expectancy has notably increased, but we need to carefully consider whether we are <u>in fact</u> better off after all.

5.5 EXERCISE 6 (page 106)

This exercise is most useful if students have not already looked at the next exercise. Possible answers:

SUGGESTED ANSWER

Fatal car accidents are increasing. This could be considered a result of increasingly powerful cars owned by inexperienced drivers.

Many people think smoking is declining among teenagers. Those that do smoke are finding it less socially acceptable to do so.

Heart attacks can happen at any age. They are, of course, more common in elderly people.

5.5 EXERCISE 7 (page 107)

GUIDELINE

Students should be building the points into complete paragraphs, adding their own ideas wherever appropriate. You may want to give only one or two to each student.

EXTENSION ACTIVITY

You could get students to divide the following passage into two body paragraphs and improve it. *They will have to add some ideas of their own.*

> Cars do not give us exercise. Car pollution causes respiratory ailments. Bicycles and walking do not. Many of the journeys could be done on foot. Some longer journeys can't. The old or the disabled have a more limited mobility. People should share cars when travelling to the same destination. More efficient public transport would help. People would use the bus if it was dependable.

Unit 5.6   Giving instructions

5.6 EXERCISE 1 (page 107)

ANSWER

Previous topic cards have focused more on presenting opinions. This card looks at describing and giving instructions.

5.6 EXERCISE 2 (page 107)

GUIDELINE

Guessing words from context is an extremely useful tool when taking the IELTS exam and in real life, too. Students may struggle so give them guidance where necessary. Encourage them to think about the kinds of words missing and logical connections.

Number 2 (laptop computer) is used twice in the answer in the students' book.

1	a piece of technology	4	After
2	laptop computer	5	then
3	first step	6	Finally

ANSWER

5.6 EXERCISE 3 (page 108)

ANSWER

> Describe how to <u>use a piece of technology</u> / <u>a piece of equipment.</u>
> You should say:
> * <u>what it is</u>
> * <u>what you use it for</u>
> * <u>how often you use it.</u>
>
> You should also explain how to <u>use it.</u>

5.6 EXERCISE 4 (page 108)

GUIDELINE

This topic card is similar to the card in *Exercise 2*, so students should be able to recycle some of the words and phrases. You may find that they are simply substituting a few words but largely copying the monologue from *Exercise 2*, in which case you may want books to be closed.

Unit 5.7   Labelling diagrams (reading)

5.7 EXERCISE 1 (page 108)

GUIDELINE

As explained in the Point of Impact, the answers are not always in the order of the text. By using the labels already attached to the diagram, students should be able to pinpoint where the answer is in the text. Remind students that they are not necessarily expected to know the vocabulary – just use the prepositions and other words to label the diagram.

ANSWER

1	Aorta	3	Right ventricle
2	Tricuspid valve	4	Left ventricle

5.7 EXERCISE 2 (page 109)

GUIDELINE

Students should be considering two key areas: (a) the labels already attached to the diagram, and (b) the prepositions used.

5.7 EXERCISE 3 (page 109)

The prepositions of place are used in *Exercise 1*. The prepositions of movement will be used in *Exercise 5*.

Some suggestions:

SUGGESTED ANSWER

Place	above, below, on top, opposite, around, in, under, beside, next to, near, behind, on the left of/right of
Movement	into, to the left of/right of, through, onto

5.7 EXERCISE 4 (page 109)

ANSWER

1	mitral valve	5	body organs	9	pulmonary valve
2	left ventricle	6	vena cava	10	pulmonary artery
3	aortic valve	7	right atrium	11	lungs
4	aorta	8	right ventricle	12	pulmonary vein

5.7 REVIEW (pages 110–111)

ANSWER

1	v	5	vi	9	NOT GIVEN	13	(thin) internal electrode
2	ix	6	iii	10	NO	14	cochlea
3	viii	7	cancer	11	sound waves	15	acoustic nerve
4	ii	8	the cost	12	bionic ear		

Unit 5.8　Tables

5.8 EXERCISE 1 (page 112)

The most important reminder here for students is not to panic when presented with a lot of data. There are more figures in the table than students are likely to have to face in the IELTS test. The main point is highlighted in the Point of Impact.

5.8 EXERCISE 2 (page 112)

a　Australian males – 77.22
　　Japanese males – 77.02
　　Japanese females – 83.35
　　Australian females – 83.23

b　South African males – 52.68
　　South African females – 56.90
　　The world figure for males – 61.00
　　The world figure for females – 65.00

c　Australians and Japanese have the highest life expectancy. South Africans have the lowest (they are the only country on the table with a lower life expectancy than that of the world population).
　　Average life expectancy for women in all countries is at least two-and-a-half years more than men, and can be as much as nearly eight years (France).

5.8 EXERCISE 3 (page 112)

Students have prepared Task I plans a number of times, but can review Unit 2.2 if necessary.

5.8 EXERCISE 4 (page 113)

a　People aged 61 + (World figure) – 8
　　People aged 61 + (Asia) – 10

b　People aged 16–60 (Asia) – 79
　　People aged 16–60 (world figure) – 76

c　North America has the highest percentage of elderly people. The world figure for under 15s is higher than the other three continents.

If students are still having difficulty preparing a plan, an intensive review of Unit 2.2 is needed.

5.8 EXERCISE 5 (page 113)

In this unit, Unit 4.8 and in Unit 6.8 students are given sample answers to Task I questions. In this unit there is a model answer. In the other two units, sample student answers are given. Ensure students are not too critical of themselves when they compare their essays with the model answer.

Unit 5.9 Unexpected questions

5.9 EXERCISE 1 (page 114)

GUIDELINE

This unit is an extension of Unit 3.9 (Misunderstandings). The answer is provided in the Point of Impact that follows.

5.9 EXERCISE 2 (page 114)

GUIDELINE

You could either have students working in pairs or you could ask the questions yourself (this would make the exercise more spontaneous).

5.9 EXERCISE 3 (page 114)

ANSWER

Encourage students to talk about a related subject if they cannot answer the question directly. The student in the example had no opinion on 'power steering' but showed valid opinions on related topics and gave the interviewer an opportunity to check his or her verbal accuracy and fluency.

5.9 EXERCISE 4 (pages 114–115)

GUIDELINE

Hopefully your students will have little to say about the topics, although you may want to think of some other ideas or get students to choose topics for their partners to talk about.

Unit 5.10 Text completion (listening)

5.10 EXERCISE 1 (page 115)

ANSWER

A Alternative medicine in the western world is often mainstream in Asian cultures. Western medicine relies on chemicals whereas alternative medicine uses more natural remedies.

B A symptom is a warning sign that a person is sick (e.g. headaches, nausea). The cause is the reason we are sick (e.g. alcohol poisoning).

5.10 EXERCISE 2 (page 115)

ANSWER

Acupuncture
Using needles to relieve stress/pressure points.

Osteopathy
The manipulation of muscles and bones to cure ailments elsewhere in the body.

Reflexology
Pressure points on the feet are massaged to heal illness elsewhere in the body.

Chemotherapy
Used to treat cancer. Chemicals are used to kill the cancer and retain healthy cells.

Surgery
Operations where the body is cut to repair or remove damaged areas.

Paediatrics
The treatment of children.

5.10 EXERCISE 3 (page 115)

a	social and political	**f**	findings
b	European Society	**g**	a long way
c	beneficial chemicals	**h**	the Greeks
d	the harmful effect	**i**	cleansing effect
e	one cigarette		

ANSWER

5.10 EXERCISE 4 (page 116)

1	the history department	**4**	thesis
2	two modules	**5**	medical backgrounds
3	in the workplace		

ANSWER

5.11 REVIEW (pages 116–117)

1	natural	**6**	10% (ten per cent)
2	muscles	**7**	C
3	the whole body	**8**	B
4	a difficult birth	**9**	emergency surgery
5	invasive	**10**	Dr Moore

ANSWER

EXTENSION ACTIVITY

In pairs, students create a short text-completion exercise based on a topic they know about. One student then gives the other the text-completion sentences and speaks about their chosen topic while the other student listens and completes the exercise.

Unit 5.11 Staying on topic

5.11 EXERCISE 1 (page 117)

If students have difficulty with this exercise, you may want to review Unit 2.5. *Topic words* (or *keywords*) are the words which tell you what subject to write about. *Task words* tell you the purpose of the essay.

SUGGESTED ANSWER

5.11 EXERCISE 2 (page 117)

Ensure students incorporate the following (as covered in Unit 3.5).

1 Identify the topic and task words.
2 Collect as many ideas (for and against) as possible.
3 Give concessions.

GUIDELINE

5.11 EXERCISE 3 (page 117)

Make sure students are aware that this is an average student's answer – they should not attempt to adopt phrases or structures without ensuring they are correct.

GUIDELINE ANSWER

GUIDELINE
ANSWER

Exactly how you approach this exercise depends on how much you want students to practise and review old lessons.

They could point out errors in vocabulary, in register or in repetition. There are also a number of useful phrases in the essay which may be worth identifying/ getting students to identify.

The essay's main failing (and its main purpose in this section) is that the second body paragraph does not answer the question, focusing more on who is to blame for addiction than the real topic.

5.11 EXERCISE 4 (page 118)

GUIDELINE

This is a basic brainstorming exercise. Some groups work better pooling ideas on the board, some work better alone (which is better practice for the test). Students should have at least 10 ideas in this section if *Exercise 5* (rows B and C) is to work properly.

5.11 EXERCISE 5 (page 118)

GUIDELINE

In the second and third row, you should further define the brainstorming area. In B, the brainstorming topic should become 'Private healthcare', and in row C it should become 'Private healthcare is unfair'. As students progress from 'Healthcare' through to 'Private healthcare is unfair', they should be rejecting some of the points they made in row A that are no longer related to the topic and adding some that are.

5.11 EXERCISE 6 (page 118)

GUIDELINE

This is a review of Unit 3.5 (preparing a plan for Task II). Students should be dividing their opinions to make paragraphs as well as preparing an introduction and rephrasing the question.

You could choose at this point to get students to write the essay.

Unit 5.12 Topic Card: Health

Refer to Teacher's notes Unit 1.12 for suggestions on using the topic card.

5.12 EXERCISE 1 (pages 118–119)

GUIDELINE

The final prompt on the card directs the topic more on to this unit (Health). In this lesson, there are some Part One questions as well as a topic card. In Unit 6.12, a topic card and some Part Three questions are given. By now, students should be building and extending these lessons much more on their own.

5.12 EXERCISE 2 (page 119)

GUIDELINE

The interviewer should make notes for Part One and Part Two. Again, students should not be overly critical of each other.

Unit 6.1	**Referencing (reading)**

6.1 EXERCISE 1 (page 120)

It refers to New Zealand.

They refers to overseas students (not just overseas students from Asia).

These factors refers to good homestay accommodation, clean and beautiful environment and cost of tuition.

6.1 EXERCISE 2 (page 120)

The completed sentences are just sample answers.

Professor Edwards has been lecturing for 16 years. <u>He</u> is very well respected by both colleagues and students.

Overseas students often find university courses difficult. <u>They</u> can find the language a major barrier to understanding.

The IELTS test is becoming increasingly popular. <u>It</u> is now held in over 100 countries.

6.1 EXERCISE 3 (page 121)

Academic overdrive?

Student life is becoming increasingly difficult. Not only are students expected to perform and compete within the class, but also to devote time and energy to extra-curricular activities as well as struggle with an increasing load of homework. The push to get into the top universities has caused many overachieving students to take on heavier workloads and more challenging classes.

<u>This push</u>, however, doesn't end once students reach university. In fact, when <u>they</u> reach the top places they have worked so hard to get into, many students are forced to work even harder than they did in high school. Once in the top universities, the pressure is on to secure a place in the top graduate school. But <u>it</u> doesn't end <u>there</u>. Once students have graduated with the best results, they find that they must continue to overextend themselves in order to secure the top jobs in their particular field. Such is the emphasis on academic success.

There are many who claim that <u>this</u> entire system is wrong because it puts too much emphasis on measuring achievement and not enough on true learning. This in turn has inevitable effects on the students themselves. In such a high-pressure learning environment, those that find the pressure overwhelming have nowhere to turn. In an academic world measured only by academic success, many students begin to feel a low sense of worth, yet they fear to turn to anyone for help as this would be perceived as a signal of failure, an inability to cope with that which other students appear to have no problem with. This can be particularly hard for foreign students as they find themselves isolated without familiar cultural or family ties in their new environment and thus they concentrate solely on their work.

Perhaps the main thing to remember is that although it is important to study hard, school life should also be fun.

Students may have slightly different answers.

ANSWER

this push	the push to get into the top universities
they	overachieving students
it	the pressure
there	at top universities
this	overachieving/overextending/pressurised (system)
those	students who have overextended themselves
this	feeling of depression, low self-esteem, nobody to talk to

6.1 EXERCISE 4 (page 121)

ANSWER

a DS
b RW
c RW

d DS
e RW

6.1 EXERCISE 5 (page 122)

Prompts are used for this exercise rather than short sentences in order to give students a little more flexibility in their answers.

SUGGESTED ANSWER

a Some schools are better than others. Consequently, those with a good reputation often have a waiting list.

b Computer technology should be used more in the class as it is becoming an essential tool in the workplace.

c A good student of English must take every opportunity to speak. In addition, they should read and listen to the language on a daily basis.

d Cambridge and Oxford are homes to world-famous universities. Furthermore, they are cities with a long history and amazing architecture.

6.1 REVIEW (pages 122–124)

ANSWER

1 i
2 iii
3 v
4 ix
5 viii
6 English language teaching
7 English-speaking country
8 Government bodies

9 NOT GIVEN
10 TRUE
11 FALSE
12 Postgraduate diploma
13 Master's degree
14 Doctorate
15 Research

Unit 6.2 Correlating data

6.2 EXERCISE 1 (page 124)

Students should be very familiar with this kind of exercise by this stage. Review Unit 2.1 if necessary.

GUIDELINE

6.2 EXERCISE 2 (page 125)

Obviously the correlation you are expected to express is between the rising cost of tuition and falling attendance.

ANSWER

6 Correlations?	Attendance fell as cost increased.

6.2 EXERCISE 3 (pages 125–126)

The aim behind this exercise is to get students thinking about why sets of data are put together when the correlation is not so clear. The first five points of each plan should now be easy for students. The main focus is on point 6 – correlations.

GUIDELINE

Set 1 The older the age bracket gets, the more people are 'Not in labour force' (together to show the changing nature of employment in increasing age).

ANSWER

Set 2 Private health insurance is directly related to income.

6.2 EXERCISE 4 (page 126)

This may be too passive an activity for some students, so you may want to move straight to *Exercise 5*.

GUIDELINE

Make sure students are aware of the Point of Impact and do not attempt to add a theory as to *why* graphs correlate.

6.2 EXERCISE 5 (page 126)

This exercise is an opportunity for them to record them for review purposes later in the course.

GUIDELINE

EXTENSION ACTIVITY

A simple extension to this would be to get students writing an essay on one of the graphs from *Exercises 2* or *3*.

Unit 6.3 Likes, dislikes and preferences

6.3 EXERCISE 1 (page 127)

As with most speaking subjects, one way of expanding what you have to say is to acknowledge a different point of view. When students state their preference for

GUIDELINE

SPEAKING SPEAKING SPEAKING SPEAKING

studying English, they should justify it and use a suitable concession word. An example is given in the Point of Impact.

6.3 EXERCISE 2 (page 127)

Ensure students are clear on the difference between likes and preferences before you begin.

ANSWER

1	B	9	C
2	C	10	C
3	A	11	A
4	C	12	B
5	B	13	B
6	A	14	A
7	B	15	C
8	A		

6.3 EXERCISE 3 (page 127)

GUIDELINE

If possible, build these short prompts into a discussion, in which students are having to defend their choices. The subjects are essentially Part One-style prompts, but they can be developed into Part Three prompts to look at them in more detail. For example, 'Learning languages' (1) could develop into discussing global communication or the impact of technology on language acquisition.

READING & LISTENING   READING & LISTENING

Unit 6.4   Discourse markers (listening)

6.4 EXERCISE 1 (page 128)

ANSWER

The linking words used make 1b and 2a the logical match.

6.4 EXERCISE 2 (page 128)

The words in bold should be recorded by students to complete the table.

ANSWER

Sentence	Next point	Linking word
1	opposite	Although …
2	sequence	next step
3	addition	not only … but also
4	concession	admittedly
5	cause/effect	as a result
6	comparison	in the same way

6.4 EXERCISE 3 (page 129)

ANSWER

You may decide to play the tape from *Exercise 5* if students are having real difficulty with this exercise.

Discourse marker	Tells you
First	There is going to be a list of points.
Like	An example is going to be given.
Anyway	This could mean a change of subject or nearing the end of the talk.
I mean	The speaker is about to rephrase or give an example.
So	An effect or a result of a previous point is about to be stated.
Moving on	Another point is going to be introduced.
As I said	The speaker is going to recap an earlier point.
To make myself clear	The speaker is going to rephrase a point.
Right	This could mean the speaker is about to begin, change the subject or is nearing the end of the talk.
To put it another way	The speaker is about to rephrase a point.
This isn't always so	The speaker is about to give exceptions to or contrasts to a previous comment.
Now	The speaker is about to begin a new subject.
Talking about that	The speaker is going to expand on a point.

6.4 EXERCISE 4 (page 129)

All of the missing words are in *Exercise 3*.

ANSWER

6.4 EXERCISE 5 (page 129)

Some alternative answers are possible. You might want to check students' answers before playing the tape.

ANSWER

1	First
2	Now
3	As I said
4	this isn't always so
5	To put it another way
6	Moving on
7	Talking about that
8	Right

6.4 EXERCISE 6 (page 130)

ANSWER

1 Falling intonation indicating end of topic.

2 Rising intonation indicating that there is more to come.

6.4 REVIEW (page 130)

ANSWER

1	C	6	10
2	cannot read	7	A
3	10	8	sounds
4	$2^{1}/_{4}$	9	spelling
5	6	10	big business

Unit 6.5 Cause and effect

6.5 EXERCISE 1 (page 131)

GUIDELINE

Students may feel they have the wrong answer as the answers to the three questions are obvious and a little repetitive.

ANSWER

1 Further education has become more accessible.

2 More people have degrees.

3 As a result.

6.5 EXERCISE 2 (page 131)

A

ANSWER

What is the cause?	an obligatory level of education
What is the effect?	illiteracy in many countries is low
What is the connector?	due to

B

What is the cause?	understanding the applications of technology has become increasingly difficult
What is the effect?	university courses are becoming increasingly specialised
What is the connector?	consequently

C

What is the cause?	the language barrier
What is the effect?	many overseas students find the first year of university courses difficult
What is the connector?	because of

D

What is the cause?	he did not get the required grade in his IELTS test

| What is the effect? | the university he had applied for rejected him |
| **What is the connector?** | thus |

E

What is the cause?	increasing problems in the education system
What is the effect?	teaching as a profession is not as prestigious as it was 50 years ago
What is the connector?	a result of

6.5 EXERCISE 3 (page 132)

This exercise should be used as an opportunity to support the Point of Impact, as well as giving students some freer practice on cause-and-effect constructions. They should be using connectors from *Exercise 2 and* their own ideas.

GUIDELINE

6.5 EXERCISE 4 (page 132)

Some constructions students could make from the diagram and the Point of Impact:

A higher standard of education has been directly affected by better teacher training, as this allows for better teachers.

As a result of better teacher training leading to better teachers, a higher standard of education has been possible.

Better teacher training, thus allowing for better teachers, has resulted in a higher standard of education.

Better teacher training results in better teachers, which in turn leads to a higher standard of education.

Given better teacher training, it follows that better teachers would mean a higher standard of education.

A higher standard of education has been indirectly affected by more funding, as this allows for more resources.

As a result of more funding leading to more resources, a higher standard of education has been possible.

More funding, thus allowing for more resources, has resulted in a higher standard of education.

More funding results in more resources, which in turn leads to a higher standard of education.

Given more funding, it follows that more resources would mean a higher standard of education.

SUGGESTED ANSWER

6.5 EXERCISE 5 (page 132)

Students should be able to brainstorm for some additional ideas as well as using *Exercise 4* to write this essay.

GUIDELINE

Unit 6.6 School life

6.6 EXERCISE 1 (page 133)

GUIDELINE

You may need to check the ages that are associated with each of the descriptions as they differ between countries. The main aim of this exercise is for students to see that there are different names and they would be able to express themselves better if they knew the system common in the country in which they are taking the test.

6.6 EXERCISE 2 (page 133)

GUIDELINE

The students' description is not intended to be a slavish copy of the example given. They should only be using this as a guideline. It is important that their description includes some personal comments – a school period they enjoyed, didn't enjoy, thought was hard, etc.

6.6 EXERCISE 3 (page 133)

GUIDELINE

The third prompt on the topic card ('what the teacher was like') asks for a brief character description. This was looked at in Unit 1.3, so you might want to review this before you begin.

Unit 6.7 Matching (reading)

6.7 EXERCISE 1 (page 134)

This is just a basic introduction to matching.

ANSWER

1 This exercise is … an example of matching.
2 Putting sentence halves together is … a common example.

6.7 EXERCISE 2 (page 134)

ANSWER

1 a   4 c
2 d   5 b
3 e

6.7 EXERCISES 3 & 4 (pages 134–135)

GUIDELINE

There are a number of different cause/effect sentences that can be used for these exercises. It is intended for students to practise not only matching but also a degree of brainstorming and speculation, as well as reviewing writing (Unit 6.5).

6.7 EXERCISE 5 (pages 135–136)

ANSWER

1 b   4 a
2 e   5 c
3 d

| Unit 6.8 | **Bar charts and pie charts** |

As with Unit 4.8, Unit 5.8 and Unit 7.8, this section is intended to give students solid practice in a specific Task I type. Unlike the other three units, two types of graph are incorporated into this section in order to review 'correlating data'. The aim remains the same: this section is intended to review applicable skills, let students look through some sample answers and then build an essay of their own which they could use as a reference guide for the future. Although students look in depth at the Task I in *Exercise 2*, you have the choice as to whether they actually write their own version.

GUIDELINE

6.8 EXERCISE 1 (page 136)

This should be an opportunity for students to prepare an introduction by using as much alternative vocabulary as possible. For example:

ANSWER

The graph shows changes in the accessibility of the Internet in two levels of school over nearly a decade.

The striking aspects from the graph could include: secondary schools were far in advance of primary for the middle section of the graph. Percentage increases in secondary schools slowed over the period; primary schools accelerated. Despite huge disparities in the middle of the graph, the difference between primary and secondary was about the same at the beginning of the period as it was at the end (about 5%).

6.8 EXERCISE 2 (page 136)

The task is clearly asking the candidate to correlate the rise in home access and school access to the Internet noting that in both cases Internet access has increased. In 1991 a higher percentage of people at home could access the Internet, although school access to the Internet was greater by the end of the period. If this exercise presented any difficulties, it may be worth reviewing Unit 6.2 (Correlating data).

ANSWER

6.8 EXERCISE 3 (page 137)

ANSWER

Topic words?	primary and secondary schools / Internet access / households
Tense?	past (1991–1999/1991/1999)
Axes?	percentage of schools / households with Internet access / years
About?	percentage of schools and percentage of households with Internet access
Trends?	more secondary schools had access / primary quickly caught up in 1997 / household access more than tripled
Correlations?	both increased from around the same point (12%) but over twice the increase for schools (90% + compared with 39% for households)

6.8 EXERCISE 4 (page 137)

It is essential that students realise these are typical students' essays, and not perfect models. The intention throughout this lesson is for students themselves to create at least the plan for a model essay.

GUIDELINE

Essay 1	Essay 2
Comment **B**	Comment **A**

EXTENSION ACTIVITY

A simple extension activity to this could be to get students to improve the sample essays.

Unit 6.9   Talking about changes

6.9 EXERCISE 1 (page 138)

GUIDELINE

You may need to do a little research on the trends before this lesson. If students don't know, then they should at least take an educated guess (and phrase it as such – 'Well, I'm not sure, but I'd imagine it must be …'). This is a good review of Unit 3.9 (Misunderstandings) and Unit 5.9 (Unexpected questions).

6.9 EXERCISE 2 (page 138)

Language expressing changes is underlined (this is partly from the writing course – 'describing trends' language, but also an introduction into other, commonly spoken, ways of expressing changes).

ANSWER

Q Tell me about recent changes in university graduation in your country.

A Well, not only in my country but also around the world, there is a <u>marked increase</u> in the number of university graduates. I can't speak for the rest of the world, but in my country this is partly due to subsidised study costs. <u>Only 10 or 15 years ago</u>, the option of going to university <u>was</u> open only to those that were wealthy enough, <u>but now</u> people from all backgrounds have an equal chance. I think this is definitely a step in the right direction, although there are still some potential students that still don't have the means.

6.9 EXERCISE 3 (page 138)

GUIDELINE

You may want to use some of the subjects from *Exercise 1* as group work before giving students time to prepare their own presentation.

a Ensure that the notes are brief.

b You should be listening for language describing changes.

Unit 6.10   Matching (listening)

This course book does not cover the subject of classifying in the listening as a separate subject. It is such a rare question type that it does not warrant a lesson of its own, but it is practised in *Exercise 3* of this lesson (Questions 1–6).

GUIDELINE

6.10   EXERCISE 1   (page 139)

1   If a question involves pictures, the skills are the same as presented in Unit 4.10 – predict not only what you might hear, but also the differences between the pictures. You could get students to talk about the language they could expect to hear as well as the differences between the pictures that may help them identify which one is being referred to.

GUIDELINE

2   For this kind of question, predicting is important but parallel phrases should also be considered. 'Different countries' could become 'other nationalities' for example.

GUIDELINE

6.10   EXERCISE 2   (page 139)

1   Joe   2   Alana   3   A

ANSWER

6.10   EXERCISE 3   REVIEW   (page 140)

1 A	6	B
2 C	7	kneeling
3 A	8	outside the school
4 A	9	pulled up
5 C	10	school badge

ANSWER

Unit 6.11   Writing a conclusion for Task II

Coming at the end of Unit 6, a section on writing a conclusion may appear a little redundant as students will already have written a number of essays. However, it incorporates many of the skills students have been acquiring so far, and allows for a useful review as well as giving students a sense of having addressed each aspect essential to the IELTS course.

GUIDELINE

6.11   EXERCISE 1   (page 140)

ANSWER

	Yes	No
a It should be at least 70 words.	X	✔
b It should include a general statement about what you have written	✔	X
c You can speculate or make a recommendation.	✔	X
d A short conclusion of 2 or 3 sentences is unacceptable.	X	✔
e There are a number of set phrases you can use in a conclusion.	✔	X

6.11 EXERCISE 2 (pages 140–141)

The wording of the titles could be a little different.

SUGGESTED ANSWER

A Advances in modern technology mean that a teacher's role in the classroom is no longer important.

B Raising the cost of university education would be beneficial as it would ensure more dedicated students.

6.11 EXERCISE 3 (page 141)

ANSWER

a R   **b** S   **c** S   **d** R

6.11 EXERCISE 4 (page 141)

SUGGESTED ANSWER

1 The number of people in higher education has increased fourfold in the past 50 years.

Raising entrance requirements would mean more educated students in smaller classes. (R)

This may well lead to a shortage of manual labour in the workplace of the future. (S)

2 Some schools cannot afford modern equipment.

The government should either divert or raise funds to equip underprivileged schools. (R)

This will lead to 'technology gaps' between schools, with some students being unprepared for an increasingly computer-dominated world. (S)

3 An increasing number of people who studied specialist courses are finding they do not have the broad scope of knowledge essential for job mobility.

An integral part of every further education course should be applicable to a wider range of jobs. (R)

This may result in companies being unable to adapt to changing economic circumstances. (S)

4 IELTS teachers are not very well paid.

They should be paid at least double their current salary as a show of appreciation for their efforts. (R)

Unless this situation is rectified, there could be a shortage of qualified teachers in the future. (S)

6.11 EXERCISE 5 (page 142)

These are signal words from *Exercises 2* and *3*.

ANSWER

To conclude,	Ultimately,
Generally speaking, therefore,	In the final analysis,
To sum up,	Overall,

Punctuation is an important aspect of these 'signal' words.

6.11 EXERCISE 6 (page 142)

For this topic, students can decide whether to end on a recommendation or a
speculation. You may want students to write the complete essay.

GUIDELINE

Unit 6.12 Topic Card: Education

Refer to Teacher's notes Unit 1.12 for suggestions on using the topic card. The
Point of Impact has already been mentioned in earlier units but is essential.

6.12 EXERCISE 1 (pages 142–143)

Make sure students are writing only brief notes.

GUIDELINE

6.12 EXERCISE 2 (page 143)

As with all such evaluation activities, make sure students are not being either too
lenient or too harsh with their colleagues. This section follows Unit 5.12, in which
students practised Part One and Part Two.

GUIDELINE

7

In the papers

Unit 7.1 Facts and opinions (reading)

7.1 EXERCISE 1 (page 144)

ANSWER

1	opinion	'convenient' is a judgement adjective
2	fact	'statistics'
3	opinion	'Some people claim'
4	fact	'research' and 'revealed'
5	opinion	'commonly accepted' is simply the opinion of the majority, not a fact.
6	fact	they **have told** the press there **will be**
7	either	Unless this statement is followed by statistics, it is an opinion. However, with statistics it could become a fact.
8	fact	'have been proven'

7.1 EXERCISE 2 (page 144)

Facts in bold. *Opinions in italics.*

ANSWER

I *personally believe* that there are such things as UFOs. The **first recorded sightings were in 1600 BC, and since then many other incidents have been reported**. Many people *exaggerate or misinterpret* what they see, but *it seems that* there certainly are genuine cases. **Statistically it is very likely that there is life on other planets** – I mean, *in my view, it would be egocentric to believe we were the only life in the universe.*

7.1 EXERCISE 3 (pages 144–145)

GUIDELINE

Encourage students to use appropriate adjectives when expressing their opinion.

7.1 EXERCISE 4 (pages 145–146)

This exercise focuses on recognising opinions.

ANSWER

a N	c P	e NG
b N	d N	f N

7.1 EXERCISE 5 (page 146)

GUIDELINE

Ideally, students should be attempting to recreate a smaller version of the text in *Exercise 4*. They need to know some facts about their subject before they can begin. Take some newspaper articles to class if you think they will be short of ideas.

EXTENSION ACTIVITY

The text in *Exercise 4* only has one type of question. Students could write different styles of questions about the topic then give their questions to a partner to answer.

Unit 7.2 **Passives**

This section is heavily grammar based, but incorporates a number of skills students should already be becoming familiar with such as transformation and academic writing. Students have already looked at using the passive to make their writing more formal.

GUIDELINE

7.2 EXERCISE 1 (page 147)

The error in A is that it uses active structures where passive structures would be more suitable. B is more suitable for academic writing.

ANSWER

7.2 EXERCISE 2 (page 147)

1 The agent is not known. (b)
2 The agent is obvious. (d)
3 The object is the focus. (a)
4 Giving a general instruction. (c)
5 A process is being described. (e)
6 The subject is long. (f)

ANSWER

7.2 EXERCISE 3 (page 148)

By adding the name of the passive, students will be more able to apply any grammar rules they have been taught.

Sentence	Construction	Passive name
1	have/ has been + past participle	present perfect
2	will + be + past participle	future
3	am / is / are + being + past participle	present continuous
4	modal + be + past participle	present / future modal
5	am / is / are + past participle	present simple
6	was / were + past participle	past simple

7.2 EXERCISE 4 (page 148)

1 The weekend papers are printed on Friday night.
2 The truth of newspaper articles is not always verified.
3 Freedom of the press should be allowed.

ANSWER

4   Newspapers will be replaced by Internet news sites.

5   Magazines have been published for over 100 years.

7.2   EXERCISE 5   (page 148)

GUIDELINE

Remind students that they should be using passive sentences where appropriate.

Unit 7.3   Film and TV

7.3   EXERCISE 1   (page 148)

GUIDELINE

This is a review of some of the sections already studied in the speaking course. The subject of TV, video and cinema should be sufficiently popular for students to extend their answers. The pointers are reviews of earlier sections (pointer a and b review Unit 4.6; pointer c and d review Unit 6.3).

7.3   EXERCISE 2   (page 148)

Some students may not agree with all the adjectives. Adjective group C, for example, is a subjective opinion. You could encourage students to give some negative adjectives after they have completed this exercise. For example, 'I think romances are boring'. Remember that they should justify their opinion.

SUGGESTED ANSWER

a Comedy   c Science fiction   e Thriller/action

b Horror   d Romance

7.3   EXERCISE 3   (page 149)

ANSWER

One way of extending your answer is to think of a particular film that fits the genre and describe that film, as explained in the Point of Impact that follows. N.B. For some students, their answer may be, 'I don't like films.' They should be able to extend that by talking about what they do like instead.

7.3   EXERCISE 4   (page 149)

GUIDELINE

This exercise extends the reviews from *Exercise 1* to add the information from Unit 2.9.

Unit 7.4   Recognising speakers (listening)

7.4   EXERCISE 1   (page 149)

GUIDELINE

Although students may remember this recording, it still serves as a useful introduction to the topic. See the tape script on pages 124–125 for answers.

7.4   EXERCISE 2   (page 149)

ANSWER

It is important in Sections 1 and 3, where there is more than one speaker. It is also an essential skill for matching questions, where students have to match a name with an opinion or comment.

7.4 EXERCISE 3 (page 149)

There are three speakers Fred, Cheryl and Wilma).

ANSWER

7.4 EXERCISE 4 (pages 149–150)

ANSWER

Wilma	thinks mobile phones are annoying.
Cheryl	suggests that they can be useful sometimes.
Fred	agrees that they can be useful.
Wilma	believes people do not respect privacy anymore.
Cheryl	does not agree that people do not respect privacy.
Fred	feels that the media in general have become too invasive.
Cheryl	claims that the public have a right to know information.

EXTENSION ACTIVITY

This is a relatively short lesson as there are relatively few skills that can be taught. If you feel students need a little more practice, then you can use other recordings in the same way as *Exercise 1*.

Unit 7.5 Predictions

7.5 EXERCISE 1 (page 150)

'Newspapers *will* be replaced' shows the speaker is confident. (A future fact in the speaker's mind.)

ANSWER

7.5 EXERCISE 2 (page 150)

a = verbs of prediction   c = adverbs of prediction
b = adjectives of prediction

ANSWER

7.5 EXERCISE 3 (page 151)

The sentences students make here are subjective, so you may want them to justify their opinions to check that they have used suitable language of prediction. This will be referred to again in *Exercise 5*.

GUIDELINE

7.5 EXERCISE 4 (page 151)

You could begin by recycling the sentences students used in *Exercise 3*, then encourage them to think of new examples.

GUIDELINE

7.5 EXERCISE 5 (page 151)

The title should lead students into using the language presented in *Exercise 2*.

GUIDELINE

Unit 7.6   Explaining effects

GUIDELINE

Before turning to the student's book, you might want to ask students if there is an event or person in their lives that has made a difference to them. This will provide a better lead-in to *Exercise 1*.

7.6 EXERCISE 1 (page 152)

ANSWER

Someone who has had a great impact has made a significant difference to your life, which is not necessarily true of someone you 'like'.

7.6 EXERCISE 2 (page 152)

GUIDELINE

You may prefer to use other situations for students to build sentences.

7.6 EXERCISE 3 (page 152)

GUIDELINE

You may want to discuss the topic card as a class before students prepare an answer.

Unit 7.7   Multiple choice (reading)

GUIDELINE

Before beginning this lesson, you could get students to discuss their views on the media in general and journalism in particular. You could begin with a discussion regarding the statement 'The public has a right to know'.

7.7 EXERCISE 1 (page 152)

ANSWER

a There are two types – completing a sentence or answering a question.
b Three or four.
c Because very often there is no grammatical or logical reason to reject any answer.
d Highlight key words, look for differences between what is being said, be careful of direct and indirect contradictions.

7.7 EXERCISE 2 (page 153)

ANSWER

B

7.7 REVIEW (pages 153–155)

ANSWER

1	D	7	TRUE
2	C	8	TRUE
3	B	9	muckraking (journalism)
4	B	10	better transportation (Better education *created* new markets. Better transportation allowed their exploitation)
5	NOT GIVEN	11	Kitchener
6	NOT GIVEN	12	television

Unit 7.8 Processes and diagrams

You could begin with a brief review of Unit 7.2 (Passives), eliciting reasons why the passive is used.

7.8 EXERCISE 1 (page 156)

In a normal Task I, the process would be given a title. However, it is clear from the diagrams that the process describes paper production.

7.8 EXERCISE 2 (page 156)

The words in bold are sequencers, showing the order the process is done in. The words in italics are in the passive. The underlined words are relative clauses. These three points are highlighted in the Point of Impact that follows.

7.8 EXERCISE 3 (pages 156–157)

The main aim of this exercise is to get students to use varied structures to describe the process. Encourage them to use sequencing words and relative clauses.

7.8 EXERCISE 4 (page 157)

This plan is a little different from other plans. It should be fairly clear what it is asking students to do. You might want students to plan the essay from *Exercise 1*.

1 Topic words?	What are the key words of the task?
2 Tense?	What tenses can I use?
3 About?	What is the process describing?
4 Begins?	Is there a clear beginning to the process?
5 Paragraph stages?	How will I divide the parts of the process into paragraphs?

7.8 EXERCISE 5 (pages 157–158)

Before moving on to this exercise, you may want to prepare a plan based on the process in *Exercise 1*.

Topic words?	process / publishing / book
Tense?	present (could also use present perfect)
About?	The stages a book goes through from writing to publication
Begins?	Clearly starts when author works on manuscript.
Paragraph stages	Pgh 1 – up to and including 'Assessment'
	Pgh 2 – pre-production to book edited and produced in galley stage
	Pgh 3 – checked by author and editor to end

WRITING
SPEAKING
SPEAKING
SPEAKING
SPEAKING
SPEAKING
READING

EXTENSION ACTIVITY

Students could brainstorm for some other subjects that may be presented as processes in the IELTS test. They could consider each unit topic individually – the water cycle, for example.

Unit 7.9   Looking at both sides

This is not the first time students have looked at being less dogmatic; this lesson is a review with some additional vocabulary.

7.9 EXERCISE 1 (page 158)

ANSWER

The candidate's answer is a little direct. It doesn't present anything as an opinion, but rather as straight facts. To be more expressive, it should include some of the vocabulary that comes in *Exercise 2*.

7.9 EXERCISE 2 (page 158)

GUIDELINE

You might want students to give you an example sentence or situation for each of the phrases, perhaps even writing them down for future reference. Some additions to the two columns could be:

Less dogmatic	Balanced
For me …	Certainly, there are other schools of thought that …
I think/I have always thought …	Other people may hold that …
My view is that …	True, …

7.9 EXERCISE 3 (page 158)

This is only one way to improve the candidate's response.

SUGGESTED ANSWER

Candidate: <u>Although it is true</u> that violence is an important problem, <u>I feel</u> that our primary concern <u>should</u> be the protection of younger viewers. In my opinion we should enforce a ban on violence on television until well after 9 p.m.

7.9 EXERCISE 4 (page 159)

GUIDELINE

You could appoint students to argue for and against each statement, practising all they have studied with regards to opinions. It may be worth pointing out that the examiner is unlikely to put them into such a direct 'argument' situation.

Unit 7.10   Gap filling (listening)

GUIDELINE

This section is largely intended as a review of a number of skills – predicting, specific information, listening in detail and most importantly text completion. You may want to prepare a number of gap-fills either from previous tape scripts in this book or from other sources.

7.10 EXERCISE 1 (page 159)

The reasons for the predictions are given in *Exercise 2*.

a	5	d	2
b	3	e	1
c	4	f	6

7.10 EXERCISE 2 (page 160)

Words in bold are from *Exercise 1*.

1 A menu, canteen, cheap food area (**£3.70** is the most expensive), students' dining hall (**burgers**), probably not a pub (no beer)

2 A business setting, possibly an inter-office e-mail or memorandum, setting up a **meeting/discussion**, important (**Head office**), a specific meeting concerning a particular **proposal**

3 Example: A hospital, hospital regulations, a noticeboard for **visitors** not patients, probably not a private ward (maximum visitor numbers and strict visiting times), probably not intensive care (visitors allowed).

4 Describes order in which something would happen, suggests a procedure that **customers** have to follow (**receive goods**), possible postal (**wait/working days**), formal or semi-formal in nature (**customer** needs to **sign form**).

5 Lecture notes, probably from a history lecture because it asks for a **famous leader/ war**, note form suggests hurried writing.

6 **University** open day – not application (**courses 'offered'**, not '**courses required**', **come and meet** but no mention of registration, specific teachers or classrooms/times).

7.10 EXERCISE 3 (page 160)

This exercise should give students the idea that some gaps in what they hear can be filled using logic and grammar skills.

a	many, today	e	signal, reading	i	world, into
b	regularly, newspaper	f	other, overtaken	j	more, age
c	world, television	g	idea, bedtime	k	read, literature
d	no, this	h	for, can		

7.10 EXERCISE 4 (page 160)

Depending on how well your students have done, you may choose to replay the tape, but remember that the recording is not particularly long, nor do students have these opportunities in the test itself.

7.10 EXERCISE 5 (page 160)

How exactly the students manage to recreate the passage is not as important as whether they have understood the essence of it and included all the pertinent details in a grammatically and logically sound format.

7.10 EXERCISE 6 (pages 160–162)

GUIDELINE

Some students may not see the value in listening to recordings they have already heard. If you feel this is the case, then it is a simple job to create a gap-fill using any other source. Recording a news bulletin from the radio and transcribing it, leaving some gaps, is good practice for both specific information and general idea. The gap-fill is from Unit 2.10, *Exercise 4*.

EXTENSION ACTIVITY

You could use any of the other tape scripts to repeat *Exercise 3* or *Exercise 6*.

Unit 7.11 Solutions

7.11 EXERCISE 1 (page 162)

ANSWER

This essay is asking for suggestions/solutions/recommendations.

7.11 EXERCISE 2 (page 162)

ANSWER

This exercise is much like Unit 2.5 (Topic and task words) in that it asks students to rephrase the title into a clearly defined question or statement.
Children are losing social skills as a result of watching too much television.

7.11 EXERCISE 3 (page 162)

GUIDELINE

Encourage students to make only notes, as they will be making fuller sentences in *Exercises 4* and *5*.

7.11 EXERCISE 4 (page 163)

GUIDELINE

In this exercise and *Exercise 5*, students will be extending their opinions from *Exercise 2*.

7.11 EXERCISE 5 (page 163)

GUIDELINE

Ensure students have read the Point of Impact before moving on to this exercise. By expanding their answer by considering the effects of their suggestions, students should be reviewing Unit 7.5 (Predictions).

7.11 EXERCISE 6 (page 163)

GUIDELINE

At this stage, students should be incorporating a number of skills into each essay. You may want students to write only a plan and then discuss their plans with you/the class/a partner.

Unit 7.12   Topic Card: The media

Refer to Teacher's notes Unit 1.12 for suggestions on using the topic card.

7.12 EXERCISE 1 (page 164)

This is a review of Unit 6.3, when students presented preferences. As with the reading, listening and writing sections of the student's book, review is becoming an increasingly large part of each lesson.

GUIDELINE

7.12 EXERCISE 2 (page 164)

You might want students to write some Part One questions before they begin the interview. More capable students could also write some Part Three questions.

GUIDELINE

Again, review is important for the topic card as students should be explaining effects (Unit 7.6).

You may choose to change the two points on which the 'interviewer' is making notes if you feel that feedback on 'areas in which the speaker is weaker' would not be constructive.

8

On the road

Unit 8.1 **Timing (reading)**

GUIDELINE

This lesson is intended to address one of the most common problems for many students – timing. They may be able to answer all the questions with accuracy, but under time pressure they do not perform so well. If possible, take a stopwatch into the class to reinforce the idea of timing, giving them regular countdowns. The stopwatches along the side of the page give an indication, but this lesson only uses two passages.

8.1 EXERCISE 1 (page 165)

ANSWER

  a FALSE

  b TRUE (although some students may argue that more time should be spent on Passage 3 than Passage 1)

  c TRUE

  d TRUE

  e FALSE

  f TRUE (this is intended as a discussion point, and to reinforce the point of the lesson)

8.1 EXERCISE 2 (page 165)

GUIDELINE

This is a test of skimming at speed. Using one text at a time, you may want to give students a time limit before asking them to close their books and talk about what they skimmed. Be aware, however, that *Exercise 3* is very similar. The texts get longer, so provide more of a challenge to skim in the same time limit.

SUGGESTED ANSWER

  A Females are statistically better drivers.

  B Younger people are less likely to drive after drinking than people aged 35 or more.

  C International travel is becoming increasingly cheap yet many people do not take advantage of it.

8.1 EXERCISE 3 (page 166)

GUIDELINE

For students that performed well in *Exercise 2*, you could get them instead to write questions based on what they remember.

8.1 EXERCISE 4 (pages 166–170)

Students should write their answers on a separate piece of paper to give some practice at transferring answers.

1 A ('D' is incorrect as the text states 'food...*would* become increasingly scarce')

2 C

3 B

4 YES

5 NO

6 NOT GIVEN

7 YES

8 NOT GIVEN ('The most recent challenge' is not necessarily the biggest danger)

9 wetlands

10 aerial obstructions

11 predators (11 and 12 can be in any order)

12 storms

13 vi

14 v

15 iii

16 i

17 viii

18 time

19 10%

20 1927

21 Labour Unions

22 Fordism

23 outsourcing

24 assembly line tasks

25 training

ANSWER

Unit 8.2 Error correction

8.2 EXERCISE 1 (pages 170–171)

The main focus of this exercise is the second row ('It should be ...'). In many ways it is irrelevant whether or not students can identify their mistakes grammatically.

GUIDELINE

ANSWER

A	Incorrect sentence	The graph shows that the percentage of total travellers using four types of transportation in three different periods.
	It should be ...	The graph shows the percentage of total travellers using four types of transportation in three different periods.
	Why?	After 'that' you need a main clause.
B	Incorrect sentence	There was a sharply increase in the number of people who attended university in 1989.
	It should be ...	There was a sharp increase in the number of people who attended university in 1989.
	Why?	'Sharply' is an adverb. You should have used an adjective to describe the noun 'increase'.
C	Incorrect sentence	The number of people who visited museums accounted for the least percentage.
	It should be ...	The number of people who visited museums accounted for the lowest percentage.
	Why?	'Percentage' is a noun. 'Least' refers to adjectives (e.g. the least popular).
D	Incorrect sentence	The beach was chosen by nearly three quarters of respondents, which was the most popular.
	It should be ...	The beach, which was the most popular, was chosen by nearly three quarters of respondents.
	Why?	The relative clause ('which was the most popular') should be close to the word it is referring to.
E	Incorrect sentence	From 1995 to 1998, the population was increased by 20% to reach nearly 150 thousand.
	It should be ...	From 1995 to 1998, the population increased by 20% to reach nearly 150 thousand.
	Why?	The passive is unnecessary.

F	Incorrect sentence	Least popular was other, which only accounted for 8%.
	It should be …	Least popular was the category marked as 'other', which only accounted for 8%.
	Why?	You can't use 'other' as you would a normal noun – it means 'a collection of everything else not mentioned'. NB. This is a common student error.
G	Incorrect sentence	It can be found that coal production dropped dramatically over the next ten years.
	It should be …	It can be seen that coal production dropped dramatically over the next ten years.
	Why?	You don't find information unless you do research and discover it. Here it is just an observation.
H	Incorrect sentence	There was a dramatic increase in hydro electric.
	It should be …	There was a dramatic increase in hydro electricity.
	Why?	'Hydro electric' is an adjective. You need the noun 'electricity'.

8.2 EXERCISE 2 (page 171)

SUGGESTED ANSWER

Copying words directly from the title, omitting plural -s, spelling errors. (Students may add more points to the list.) At this point, it is worth asking students when they think is the right time to correct these errors. Recommend they do so after they have finished Task II, as more points would be lost if a student hadn't managed to complete his or her second task.

8.2 EXERCISE 3 (pages 171–172)

GUIDELINE

You may want students to refer to Unit 4.8 and 6.8 to see what kind of report they should be preparing. Using essays written by your own students may actually be more effective for this exercise. The underlined sections are errors.

ANSWER

> This illustration shows the number of citizens who used different transportation to work in 3 separated years, namely 1990 1995 and 2000 in Melingen City. The vertical axes represent the number of people from zero to 100 in thousands. The horizontal one stands for 6 different modes of transport: buses, cars, train, bicycles and other.
>
> The number of people who drive to work was dramatically higher than the others. The number of citizens who went to work by bus was 20 000 in 1990 it rose to 25 000 in 1995 then dropt to 20 000 in 2000. In contrast the number of people who travelled by train was slightly higher than the people travelled by bus. The number was approximate 26 000 in 1990. The number of people who travelled by train which was 36 000 was the highest.
>
> The number of people who transported by bicycle was not high.
>
> To sum up, the bar chart shows that cars were the most popular form of transport over the 3 years and less people went to work on feet.
>
> (174 words)

SUGGESTED ANSWER

Students should also note in their report that there is no variety with regards to the statistics, the language is at times not academic, and the essay seems very hurried towards the end.

9.2 EXERCISE 4 (page 172)

You may want to encourage students to follow their own style of writing, or you may get them to simply rewrite the essay with basic corrections.

GUIDELINE

EXTENSION ACTIVITY

A relatively simple exercise would be to get students reviewing either their own or other students' old essays.

Unit 8.3   Travel

8.3 EXERCISE 1 (page 172)

Some potential Part One questions on this topic are used in *Exercise 2*.

GUIDELINE

8.3 EXERCISE 2 (page 173)

Question 7 may be confusing for students studying in their own country.

ANSWER

1	How has travel changed	**c**	in your country over the past 20 years?
2	What's your ideal	**f**	kind of holiday?
3	What do you do	**b**	on holiday?
4	What is the road system	**g**	like in your country?
5	Do you	**a**	enjoy travelling?
6	What countries would	**e**	you like to visit?
7	How does travel here and	**d**	in your country compare?

8.3 EXERCISE 3 (page 173)

Skill A	= 3	Skill C	= 2	Skill E	= 5	Skill G	= 1
Skill B	= 4	Skill D	= 7	Skill F	= 6		

ANSWER

8.3 EXERCISE 4 (page 173)

This is a review of Unit 6.9.

Interviewer:	How has travel changed in your country over the past twenty years?
Candidate:	*Well, the first thing is that there are <u>more and more</u> cars on the road, so traffic congestion <u>is becoming a serious issue</u>. We <u>used to have</u> a good public transport system, <u>but</u> fewer people use it <u>now</u> so the services <u>have been reduced</u>.*

ANSWER

8.3 EXERCISE 5 (page 173)

You could get students to write their answers to two or three of the questions first, making sure that they are extending their answers as much as would be natural. Again, question 7 is irrelevant for students studying in their own country.

GUIDELINE

Unit 8.4　Meaning and intonation (listening)

8.4　EXERCISE 1　(page 174)

GUIDELINE

This exercise is a review of former units.

8.4　EXERCISE 2　(page 174)

ANSWER

1　not unusual　　　　2　misconception　　　　3 not unlike

8.4　EXERCISE 3　(page 174)

The intonation for this is very important.

ANSWER

1 B　　2　A　　3 B　　4 B　　5 A　　6 A　　7 B

8.4　EXERCISE 4　(page 174)

GUIDELINE

Students may have difficulty with intonation in this exercise. Remind them that it is good practice for the speaking test.

8.4　EXERCISE 5　(page 175)

ANSWER

1	B	4	433 398	7	recommended	10	N
2	B	5	VN217	8	Gold Star		
3	Jackson	6	20	9	$54		

Unit 8.5　Commonly confused words

GUIDELINE

You have probably already addressed any recurring vocabulary errors, but this lesson highlights some of the more common examples. This lesson would be better if there were some commonly confused words particular to your students.

8.5　EXERCISE 1　(page 176)

ANSWER

a　*Such* is followed by a noun. *So* is followed by the adjective alone.

b　*Fewer* is for countable nouns. *Less* is for uncountable nouns.

c　Use the word *humans* only if you are highlighting the difference between humans and other animals.

d　*Economic* means related to the economy. *Economical* means cheap or good value.

e　You cannot use *percentage* and a number. *Percentage* is used for talking generally.

f　*Information* is a fact or knowledge about a specific event or subject. *Knowledge* means having information and understanding it through experience.

g　As a verb, *effect* means put into action. *Affect* means cause a change in something.

h　*Global* means around the whole world. *International* means between nations or countries.

8.5　EXERCISE 2　(page 176)

ANSWER

a	such	c	economical	e	percentage
b	people	d	effect	f	fewer

8.5 EXERCISE 3 (page 177)

It is possible that students are not aware of the words they personally confuse, in which case they can talk about words they know but think a lower-level student would have difficulty with.

GUIDELINE

8.5 EXERCISE 4 (page 177)

Students should be able to recycle the words that have arisen during this lesson. Again, seeing a plan before students actually begin to write may help you give some advice.

GUIDELINE

EXTENSION ACTIVITY

You can select some academic vocabulary. Students use a dictionary to write example sentences.

Unit 8.6 Recounting an experience

As an introduction to this lesson, you could talk about how students felt on their first day studying IELTS.

GUIDELINE

8.6 EXERCISE 1 (page 177)

Students may not be too comfortable talking about (d) – a time when they felt embarrassed. However, they could potentially have to talk about something similar in the test, so remind them that they can use their imagination.

GUIDELINE

8.6 EXERCISE 2 (page 177)

This exercise is intended to highlight the Point of Impact that follows. It should be relatively easy as thinking of what to say requires only an average memory.

GUIDELINE

8.6 EXERCISE 3 (page 178)

ANSWER

The <u>best</u> holiday I have ever been on was a three-week trip to the South of Spain. The people were <u>very friendly</u> and the weather was <u>absolutely fabulous</u>, with bright blue skies every day. It was <u>one of the cleanest</u> environments I've ever experienced – there didn't seem to be any pollution, and that's a <u>welcome change</u> compared with my hometown.

8.6 EXERCISE 4 (page 178)

Students have already looked at how useful adjectives are in speaking. This exercise and *Exercise 5* extends this into adverbs. You may want to write the adverbs on the board so students can choose or they may be able to complete the exercise without help.

GUIDELINE

A – absolutely
B – completely

C – severely
D – terribly

SUGGESTED ANSWER

8.6 EXERCISE 5 (page 178)

GUIDELINE

The six prompts should give students plenty of ideas to talk about, again reviewing as much as possible from previous lessons. However, it is important that students do not sound like they have rehearsed their subjects – it is very important to maintain a natural intonation.

Unit 8.7 Classifying (reading)

GUIDELINE

As a lead-in, you could get students considering the advantages and disadvantages of different modes of transport.

8.7 EXERCISES 1 & 2 (page 178)

ANSWER

Exercise 1 is a matching exercise. *Exercise 2* is a classifying exercise.

		Complete sentence	C/M/PT
Sentence 1	a	Being tied to a timetable and schedule, it is often inconvenient.	PT
Sentence 2	c	It offers a freedom some argue cannot be found with four wheels.	M
Sentence 3	e	Its advantage is that it can seat the average family quite comfortably.	C
Sentence 4	d	Despite the restrictions, this is the most environmentally friendly option.	PT
Sentence 5	b	An increasing number of households have two, despite the cost.	C

8.7 EXERCISE 3 (page 179)

ANSWER

Public transport	Cars	Motorbikes
rigidity of the timetable the inflexibility of destination concerns about getting a seat waiting at bus stops or train stations, having the correct change keeping our tickets perceived prejudices and opinions notion of freedom	symbolises more than just convenience	symbolises more than just convenience a way to recapture our lost youth less common and less polluting not practical open to the elements, is at greater risk, has no practical carrying capacity or the luxury of a heater or CD player

8.7 EXERCISE 4 (page 179)

ANSWER

This exercise only asks whether it is a classification question or not (it is), leading into the Point of Impact that follows.

8.7 EXERCISE 5 (page 179)

ANSWER

TRUE, FALSE, NOT GIVEN-style questions are also a form of classification.

8.7 EXERCISE 6 (page 180)

ANSWER

Given the number of people giving opinions, it would be reasonable to assume that you will be asked to classify who said what.

8.7 EXERCISE 7 (page 181)

1 EM	3 ML	5 ML	7 JU
2 DM	4 EM	6 ML	8 EM

ANSWER

Unit 8.8   Appropriate language

Much of this section is actually a review of what students have already studied, at least in part. However, this is an opportunity for you to address any persistent errors that students may have as well as introduce some additional points.

GUIDELINE

8.8 EXERCISE 1 (page 181)

This paragraph is not concise. It only conveys the information that space exploration is expensive, as explained in the Point of Impact that follows.

ANSWER

8.8 EXERCISE 2 (page 181)

Road rage is one symptom of our obsession with speed. Irritation and anger are common when we find ourselves having to wait for anything, regardless of whether we have any reason to hurry.

SUGGESTED ANSWER

8.8 EXERCISE 3 (page 182)

a   Does not connect sentences.
b   Addresses the examiner directly.
c   Exclamation marks should be avoided (this will be covered again in Unit 9).
d   Avoid rhetorical questions.
e   The subject should not be at the end of such long sentences.

ANSWER

8.8 EXERCISE 4 (page 182)

This is a very short introduction to the subject of inversion. If you find that students have little difficulty, then you could extend this with some additional work. If it appears to be causing students some problems, then it is probably better to avoid it as there is very little time left in which students can practise applying it.

GUIDELINE

a   Seldom are those who sell drugs caught and punished.
b   So serious is the situation becoming that governments are enforcing stricter penalties.
c   Without a concerted effort, the environment will not repair itself.

ANSWER

8.8 EXERCISE 5 (page 182)

As with all of the essays so far, academic writing must be stressed. It may prove worthwhile to brainstorm and write the essay as a group, with each student contributing a sentence which is improved on by other students until it has become as academic as possible.

GUIDELINE

Unit 8.9 Speculating

GUIDELINE

Before beginning this lesson you may want to review Unit 7.5 for the language of predictions.

8.9 EXERCISES 1–3 (page 183)

GUIDELINE

These exercises are drawing attention to conditional sentences. As explained in the Point of Impact, any speculation students make should be justified. As with 'inversion' in Unit 8.8, you could use additional exercises on conditional sentences if you feel it is necessary. In *Exercise 3* the difference is degree of probability. Deforestation probably will be allowed to continue but passports probably won't be abolished.

8.9 EXERCISE 4 (page 183)

GUIDELINE

The four phrases given are other useful ways of speculating in the speaking test. You can either think of new situations in which to apply these sentences, or simply get students to repeat their opinions from *Exercises 1* and *2* with the new vocabulary. You will be using them again in *Exercise 5*.

8.9 EXERCISE 5 (page 183)

GUIDELINE

In this exercise, students should be using all their academic skills. They should also be able to think of some situations in which speculation is required.

Unit 8.10 Labelling maps and plans (listening)

GUIDELINE

You may want to review Unit 4.10 (labelling objects) before beginning this lesson. This lesson focuses on some of the same skills.

8.10 EXERCISE 1 (page 184)

ANSWER

Diagram A is a floor plan. Diagram B is a map. Students that read the title of this section should be able to answer easily.

8.10 EXERCISE 2 (page 184)

ANSWER

Prepositions (place and movement) are very important when labelling maps and plans in the listening.

8.10 EXERCISE 3 (page 184)

GUIDELINE

In this exercise, students should be able to construct sentences using prepositions of place. You might want them to describe how to get from one building to another, with other students following the description and giving the name of the building at which the description arrives.

8.10 EXERCISE 4 (page 185)

1 Reception	4 Theory test room B	7 Practice test area
2 Toilet	5 Processing office	
3 Theory test room A	6 Waiting area	

8.10 EXERCISE 5 (page 185)

Students should be giving detailed descriptions, not basic sentences. You may find it more productive to use another floor plan for this exercise, something that is familiar to students.

8.10 REVIEW (pages 185–186)

1 mentor	5 business studies	9 meet students
2 no	6 A	10 7.30
3 meeting people	7 library	
4 no	8 plays volleyball	

Unit 8.11 Editing

8.11 EXERCISE 1 (pages 186–187)

This first exercise is very similar to Unit 8.2 (Error correction Task I).

Incorrect sentence	Fining industries that are guilty of polluting the atmosphere is not the only.
It should be …	Fining industries that are guilty of polluting the atmosphere is not the only solution to the problem.
Why?	*Only* must be followed by a noun.
Incorrect sentence	The most beautiful future will come to those who are worthy.
It should be …	The environment in the future will be better if we take care of it.
Why?	You are writing for the IELTS, not for a poetry book.
Incorrect sentence	In my opinion, nuclear power becomes the main source for our energy needs.
It should be …	In my opinion, nuclear power should/will/might become the main source for our energy needs.
Why?	If you are giving an opinion, make sure you use appropriate language.
Incorrect sentence	In the future, developments in the medicality will greatly extend our life span.
It should be …	In the future, development in medicine will greatly extend our life span.
Why?	Don't try to impress the examiner with 'academic'-sounding vocabulary if you are not sure.
Incorrect sentence	During a war, many public buildings are devasted.
It should be …	During a war, many public buildings are devastated.
Why?	Spelling errors can make your meaning unclear.

Incorrect sentence	Developments in the computer industry continue to accelerate, almost to the point of being beyond our ability to continually learn and assimilate these new technologies and therefore unless we make a conscious effort to reduce the quantity and instead invest more in the quality we will find ourselves entirely swamped with a mass of almost instantly obsolete hardware and software….
It should be …	About three sentences!
Why?	Writing long, complex sentences is only an IELTS skill if you can do it well. Otherwise, short sentences are better!
Incorrect sentence	Nuclear power, which is used widely throughout the world, has many positive and negative aspects and we should consider them all before we pursue a particular course of action because there are alternatives and furthermore, these
It should be …	Who knows?!
Why?	Your examiner must be able to read your essay if he or she is going to mark it!

8.11 EXERCISE 2 (page 187)

This is intended to be a fairly light-hearted look at editing.

ANSWER

a   Verbs ~~has~~ <u>have</u> to be in the correct person

b   ~~And~~ don't start a sentence with 'and' or 'but'.

c   Avoid clichés, even if ~~every coin has two sides~~ <u>you think there are</u> <u>different opinions</u>.

d   ~~No sentence fragments.~~ <u>Sentence fragments should be avoided</u>.

e   Make sure you are clear when you are ~~not~~ using ~~no~~ double negatives.

f   Be careful not to overuse commas in your writing.

g   ~~DO NOT~~ <u>Do not</u> emphasise your opinion with capital letters.

h   ~~Should rhetorical questions be used?~~ <u>Rhetorical questions should not be</u> <u>used</u>.

i   Exaggeration will not ~~make your essay a billion times better~~ <u>improve your</u> <u>essay</u>.

j   Edit carefully in case <u>you</u> have forgotten something.

8.11 EXERCISE 3 (page 188)

The reasons for the best paragraphs are given in *Exercise 4*.

ANSWER

1 B   2 A   3 B   4 B   5 A

8.11 EXERCISE 4 (page 188)

ANSWER

a   i and b   d   e and c

b   a and g   e   d and f

c   h and j

8.11 EXERCISE 5 (page 189)

ANSWER

Only the type of error has been highlighted here as corrections can take many forms. Students may also find errors in the style of the essay.

	GUIDELINE

As the number of private cars _increases_, so has the level of pollution. Over-reliance on cars at the expense of public transport _have_ made this problem even _bigger_, causing many concerned citizens to look for a solution to the problem.

grammar
grammar
vocabulary

One potential solution to the problem is to discourage the use of private cars by raising taxes. If the cost of petrol was increased, then many people _will consider_ using alternative forms of transport or even walking. _Admittedly_, there would be a number of complaints from car drivers, but these would not be _worthy_ when balanced against the environmental benefits

grammar/spelling

vocabulary

Another solution could be to look at more specific causes of the problem. Modern cars are fitted with cleaner burning engines and catalytic converters. _Furthermore_, they do not cause as much of an environmental hazard as some older cars. In Japan, for example, cars are heavily taxed once _they've_ been on the road for three years or more, encouraging people to buy new cars which pollute less. By heavily taxing older vehicles from the road, some of the worst _pollution making_ vehicles would be taken off the road. _Admittedly_, this would not really be fair to those who cannot afford a new car with such regularity.

incorrect linking word
register

vocabulary/repetition of linking word

An improvement in the quality and _effishiency_ of public transport would also encourage people to use _there_ cars less. In London, a system has been operating for some time in which people are allocated days of the week when they can use their cars. On days _what_ they are not allowed to drive, public transport is taken. _London is also a difficult place to get around, especially for visitors. London taxi drivers have a worldwide reputation for their ability to navigate the main roads and the back streets with equal ease, the result of having to take an extensive test based on the local road system._

spelling
spelling/grammar

grammar
off topic

Although these are potential solutions to the problem, none of them are _perfection_. Only by a concerted effort by both the government and the public can this situation truly be resolved.

vocabulary

Unit 8.12 Topic Card: Transport

Refer to Teacher's notes Unit 1.12 for suggestions on using the topic card.

8.12 EXERCISE 1 (page 189)

By talking about a memorable journey, students should be considering many of the lessons they have covered – opinions, justification, explaining effects, recounting an experience, describing likes and dislikes, preferences, comparatives and superlatives, etc.

GUIDELINE

8.12 EXERCISE 2 (pages 189–190)

This is the final topic card that will be used as classwork. You may choose to focus only on this, or you may want to get students brainstorming for Part One and Part Three questions before you begin.

GUIDELINE

8.12 EXERCISE 3 (page 190)

By having a checklist of skills, students should have a clear idea of what is expected of them. You may want to brainstorm for more before students begin the exercise.

GUIDELINE

9

Looking ahead

| Unit 9.1 | **Review of reading skills** |

9.1 EXERCISE 1 (page 191)

GUIDELINE

As you will read a number of times in this unit, the main purpose of the lessons from this point on should be to give students *confidence*. In this exercise, it is important that any comments made are constructive and not over-critical. The most common answers are vocabulary and the amount of time.

9.1 EXERCISE 2 (page 191)

Students should be able to answer these questions without any difficulty.

ANSWER

1 3
2 No
3 Move on and come back if there's time at the end. Always write *something* in the answer booklet.
4 No (very important!)

9.1 EXERCISE 3 (pages 191–193)

GUIDELINE

You may want to go back and review the Points of Impact from the reading sections before you begin this. In Text 1 and 2, most question types are referred to. The skills which should be used can all be found in the lessons relevant to the question. For example, for Questions 1 to 3, the skills are presented in Unit 4.7.

9.1 EXERCISE 4 (pages 194–196)

ANSWER

Text 1		Text 2	
1	FALSE	1	Cocaine
2	NOT GIVEN	2	Anabolic steroids
3	TRUE	3	Relaxants
4	b	4	Mask pain
5	c	5	short careers
6	e	6	drug testing
7	a	7	natural advantage
8	d	8	evade detection
9	B	9	inaccuracy
10	C	10	allegations

Unit 9.2   Review of Task I skills

Before beginning this Unit, it may be useful to get students looking through the writing course and reviewing the Points of Impact.

GUIDELINE

9.2 EXERCISES 1–4 (pages 196–199)

This is similar to Unit 9.1 in which students reviewed the skills necessary for different question types in the reading test. The aim of these titles is to make sure all students know the skills needed.

GUIDELINE

EXTENSION ACTIVITY

You could get students to make short notes outlining the skills that are needed for each type of Task I.

Unit 9.3   Plans and ambitions

By now, you should be able to estimate your students' abilities, but be aware that, for some students, this could become more of a grammar presentation than a speaking lesson. You might want to elicit the difference between a plan and an ambition before you begin.

GUIDELINE

9.3 EXERCISE 1 (page 198)

'Going to' (talking about arranged plans). At this point, you may decide to use some supplementary grammar material.

ANSWER

9.3 EXERCISE 2 (page 198)

Well, I'd love to get a job working with children, so I'm planning to take a teacher training course. I wouldn't mind working abroad for a while, but I expect that will have to wait until I get some experience. I'd love to do some voluntary work though – that would give me an opportunity to travel as well as get some experience of a different culture. I'm hoping to complete the course within the next year because I want to start work as soon as possible.

ANSWER

9.3 EXERCISE 3 (page 198)

Students should be able to use all the vocabulary presented above to answer this question, but if they are having any difficulty then you could move on to *Exercise 4*.

GUIDELINE

9.3 EXERCISE 4 (page 198)

You may need to be more specific for some students. For example, plans and ambitions regarding your career, your personal life, your financial situation.

GUIDELINE

Unit 9.4   Review of listening skills

9.4 EXERCISE 1 (page 199)

GUIDELINE

Opinions will probably vary between students, but any opinion is acceptable assuming it is sufficiently justified. However, predicting and anticipating should be in everyone's top three.

9.4 EXERCISE 2 (page 199)

GUIDELINE

Prediction skills are essential. Make sure that students have done as much as they can before you play the recording. Students should also remember that when predicting, they are looking for the *type* of word missing, not necessarily the actual answer.

9.4 EXERCISE 3 (page 200)

ANSWER

The questions should give the information that there are at least two people – the interviewer and Dr Philipps. The subject is something about a book.

9.4 EXERCISE 4 (page 200)

ANSWER

1 *Silver Lining*	5 Area 51	9 (alien) abductions
2 sceptical	6 MacBrazel	10 £19.99
3 C	7 a UFO	
4 C	8 conspiracy theorists	

9.4 EXERCISES 5–6 (page 200)

Having just practised predicting skills, this exercise reviews note-taking skills.

ANSWER

1 Two	5 six hours	9 a camera
2 appropriately	6 provided	10 the plants
3 good footwear	7 7.00 a.m.	
4 a change of clothes	8 traffic	

Unit 9.5   Review of Task II skills

9.5 EXERCISE 1 (page 200)

GUIDELINE

The following numbers are a guide only. There are some sections that students may number differently, but as with any such difference they should justify their reasons.

SUGGESTED ANSWER

8	Start writing
2	Identify the topic
5	Brainstorm for ideas
4	Divide the question into two parts (if appropriate)
3	Identify the task words
6	Remove irrelevant ideas
9	Edit your work
7	Organise your ideas into paragraphs
1	Read the question

9.5 EXERCISE 2 (page 201)

Students should be building a plan, following the skills they have used many times throughout the course.

GUIDELINE

9.5 EXERCISE 3 (pages 201–202)

For some of the paragraphs it is clear which is superior (in the second paragraph, for example, candidate B has the better answer). However, for other paragraphs it is simply a matter of choice. You may find it easier to discuss each paragraph in turn rather than reading everything.

GUIDELINE

EXTENSION ACTIVITY

By using students' essays from earlier in the course, you could get them to decide which is superior and why. You may need to type their essays so that students are concentrating on the language, not trying to identify the author via the handwriting. This works well if you have asked students to e-mail the work to you.

Unit 9.6   Review of speaking skills

9.6 EXERCISE 1 (page 202)

At this stage, you may already have areas which you think your student needs to practise. This lesson focuses on general speaking skills. By speaking about the topic based on the skills, you should have the opportunity to review most areas.

GUIDELINE

9.6 EXERCISE 2 (page 202)

Having prepared some notes, students should be able to think of not only areas to talk about, but also points of discussion or debate as well as topic cards and Part Three-style questions.

GUIDELINE

Unit 9.7   Test

If this is the first time students have looked at a complete test, there will be a few points they will be unfamiliar with.

1 Listening tests are often divided.

GUIDELINE

2 There are generally only two or three different question types for each listening, with a pause in the recording when different question styles are being used.

3 The narrator will often speak in the pauses between question styles.

1	Waddell	6	$35
2	(07) 263 8666	7	unlimited kilometres
3	Visa card	8	relatives
4	Robyn Place	9	an automatic
5	10	10	driving licence

ANSWER

ANSWER

11	681	26	40 litres
12	tunnels	27	solar coil
13	5	28	20
14	X	29	65
15	whale watching	30	rigid foam
16	Indian Pacific	31	services marketing
17	early settlers	32	legal advice
18	millionth	33	weakness
19	states	34	customer numbers
20	the continent	35	tangible
21	B	36	expectations
22	B	37	clients
23	C	38	constantly improve
24	A	39	conduct surveys
25	A	40	A representative

IELTS test: Reading

ANSWER

1	C	21	voluntary support services
2	G	22	vii
3	E	23	iv
4	F	24	ix
5	B	25	v
6	H	26	ii
7	D	27	x
8	A	28	viii
9	headboard	29	ix
10	weight	30	iv
11	pendulum	31	vi
12	bellows	32	i
13	cheaper	33	NOT GIVEN
14	accurate	34	NO
15	moving parts	35	NO
16	A	36	YES
17	C	37	NO
18	melatonin	38	facts
19	less sunlight	39	job mobility
20	light therapy	40	more discretion

Unit 9.8   Test

GUIDELINE

A useful way to mark students' Task II essays would be to use the writing guide found in the back of the *Teacher's Guide*.

Unit 9.9   Test

If possible, another teacher should be the interviewer for the speaking test. It often helps to have a fresh perspective, especially if you have been teaching the same student(s) for some time.

GUIDELINE

Unit 9.10   On your marks ...

As this is the last section of the book, much of the lesson should be spent in overcoming one of the most common obstacles to a good IELTS result – lack of confidence. You could open the lesson with a discussion about exam nerves and how to deal with them. Different nationalities often have different approaches with regard to exam stress.

GUIDELINE

9.10 EXERCISE 1 (page 214)

This is an extension of the lead-in to the section. There is no definite right or wrong answer at this point. It is more an opportunity for students to see that exam nerves are not an unusual phenomena and that there are techniques which can be used to overcome them.

GUIDELINE

9.10 EXERCISE 2 (page 215)

The reading in *Exercise 2* is not particularly challenging and the answers can be located (deliberately) easily. Again, the main purpose of this section is to increase student confidence.

ANSWER

1 C   3 C   5 C
2 B   4 A   6 D

9.10 EXERCISE 3 REVIEW (pages 215–217)

1 nervous   6 A
2 B   7 Task I
3 spelling   8 Passage 2
4 Interview Room 5 9 multiple choice
5 B   10 C

ANSWER

Unit 9.11   Get set ...

These are the main points that should be impressed upon students at this stage:

GUIDELINE

a Confidence is very important.
b There is time in the test to apply the skills they have learned.
c Relying on a particular topic and gearing all their energies towards it is not a good idea.

As with the Reading and Listening part of the book (in which students look at some tips for the night before the test), this final section is intended as a confidence booster. The idea behind getting students to plan but not write the essays is that they should be able to review some of the more important points with a slightly more relaxed approach.

9.11 EXERCISES 1 & 2 (pages 217–218)

GUIDELINE

At this point in the course, you will know the best way for you to approach these exercises. By arranging classes into small groups wherever possible, students should be able to pool ideas on answering both Task I and II. Alternatively you may find that some students work better alone, but the main aim is to make sure all students contribute something.

The main focus of this lesson is not to get students producing completed writing tasks (there may not be time to mark them and return them in time for them to actually serve any real purpose). *Exercises 1* and *2* are primarily intended as a light review of the book and a platform for discussion and brainstorming. You may want to brainstorm other topics or look back at the essay titles studied throughout the course.

Unit 9.12 ... Go

SUGGESTED ANSWER

9.12 EXERCISE 1 (page 218)

Simplicity	If in doubt, keep what you are trying to say simple. It's better to be accurate than misunderstood.
Pronunciation	Obviously important!
Ease	When you are being interviewed, relax!
Attitude	Be friendly and polite.
Knowledge	You have completed this course so you are ready for the test – believe in yourself.
Intonation	Try to sound interested and interesting.
Natural	All you are doing is speaking – just speak like you do to your teacher. Be natural!
Go	You know how hard you've worked. Go and get the best result you can.

9.12 EXERCISE 2 (page 219)

GUIDELINE

The topic card is intended only as a forum for conversation and shouldn't really be used as a proper topic card (it is an unlikely subject for the test).

Appendices

You can photocopy this page.

Noun	Person	Verb	Passive?	Adjective	Adverb	Meaning

You can photocopy this page.

The title:
The rephrased question:

plan	_____ _____ _____ _____ _____ _____ _____ _____ _____ _____ _____ _____ _____ _____ _____ _____	Topic words?	
		Task words?	
		Paragraph ideas?	
Intro:	_____ _____ _____ _____ _____ _____ _____ _____ _____	Have I avoided copying words from the title?	
		Have I shown the reader what I'm going to say?	
Body paragraph 1	_____ _____ _____ _____ _____ _____ _____ _____ _____ _____ _____ _____	Topic sentence?	
		Justifying points/evidence?	
		Concession/qualification?	
		Relevant vocabulary?	
		Linking words?	
		Complex sentences/variety of tenses?	

	Answered the question?	
	Clear and concise?	
	Edited?	
Body paragraph 2	Topic sentence?	
	Justifying points/evidence?	
	Concession/qualification?	
	Relevant vocabulary?	
	Linking words?	
	Complex sentences/variety of tenses?	
	Answered the question?	
	Clear and concise?	
	Edited?	
Conclusion	Relevant vocabulary?	
	Summarised main points?	
	(Re-)stated your opinion?	
	Speculated or recommended?	
	Edited?	

Listening tape scripts

Listening **1.4** EXERCISE **3**

> **a** Edmund Hillary, that's E-D-M-U-N-D H-I-L-L-A-R-Y, was born in Auckland, that's spelt A-U-C-K-L-A-N-D.
>
> **b** Katherine Mansfield, that's K-A-T-H-E-R-I-N-E M-A-N-S-F-I-E-L-D, was born in Wellington, that's spelt W-E-L-L-I-N-G-T-O-N.
>
> **c** Alexander Aitken, that's A-L-E-X-A-N-D-E-R A-I-T-K-E-N, was born in Dunedin, that's spelt D-U-N-E-D-I-N.
>
> **d** Te Rangi Hiroa, that's T-E R-A-N-G-I H-I-R-O-A, was born in Wairarapa, that's spelt W-A-I-R-A-R-A-P-A.
>
> **e** Kate Sheppard, that's K-A-T-E S-H-E-P-P-A-R-D, was born in Liverpool, that's spelt L-I-V-E-R-P-O-O-L.
>
> **f** Ernest Rutherford, that's E-R-N-E-S-T R-U-T-H-E-R-F-O-R-D, was born in Brightwater, that's spelt B-R-I-G-H-T-W-A-T-E-R.
>
> **g** Colin Murdoch, that's C-O-L-I-N M-U-R-D-O-C-H, was born in Timaru, that's spelt T-I-M-A-R-U.
>
> **h** John Britten, that's J-O-H-N B-R-I-T-T-E-N, was born in Christchurch, that's spelt C-H-R-I-S-T-C-H-U-R-C-H.

Listening **1.4** EXERCISE **6**

Jane Kinsella	Hi.
ATC Receptionist	Good morning. Can I help you?
Jane Kinsella	Yes, I'd like to enrol in your business course.
ATC Receptionist	Well, we run two business courses here, the BA and the MBA. Which course were you interested in?
Jane Kinsella	I don't have a degree, so I won't be able to study the MBA.
ATC Receptionist	That's right. OK, if you'd like to give me some details, I'll complete an application form and someone from the Business Department will contact you directly. First, what's your name?
Jane Kinsella	Jane Kinsella.
ATC Receptionist	Kinsella? Could you spell that for me?
Jane Kinsella	Hm. It's K-I-N-S-E-L-L-A.
ATC Receptionist	OK, and how old are you, Jane?
Jane Kinsella	Well, my date of birth is the 4th of August 1982.
ATC Receptionist	Good, thanks. Can you tell me where you're from?
Jane Kinsella	I'm from Britain.
ATC Receptionist	And where do you live now?
Jane Kinsella	Number 32 Maich Road, Auckland.
ATC Receptionist	Can you spell your road name for me?
Jane Kinsella	Yes, it's M – A – I – C – H.
ATC Receptionist	Right, thank you. Do you have a contact number?
Jane Kinsella	Only a mobile. It's 021 455 7326.
ATC Receptionist	And what are you doing now?

Jane Kinsella	Well, I was working in a shop until two weeks ago, but at the moment I'm not doing anything.
ATC Receptionist	Good, now if we can move on to your education. Do you have any qualifications?
Jane Kinsella	As I said, I don't have a degree, but I do have 4 'A' levels.
ATC Receptionist	I'll write that down. So your ideal choice is to study the BA in Business Studies, is that right?
Jane Kinsella	Yes, that's right. If I can't enrol in that course I'll wait until the next intake.
ATC Receptionist	OK, so no second choice of study. Tell me, why do you want to study the BA in Business?
Jane Kinsella	Well, I'm very interested in becoming self-employed at some time in the future, but I need some experience in a larger company first and they won't accept people without a BA.
ATC Receptionist	Hmm. And how will you pay for the course?
Jane Kinsella	I'll use my savings for most of the course, and if I have any problems I'll take a part-time job, but I hope I won't have to.
ATC Receptionist	That's fine – I'll just write 'savings'. And now a final question. Do you mind if I ask you why you want to study here?
Jane Kinsella	Not at all. Your course was actually recommended by a friend. He's in his second year now but he thinks it's very good.
ATC Receptionist	OK, that's great. I'll hand your application to the Admissions Office and they'll contact you from there.
Jane Kinsella	Thanks very much. Bye.

Listening 1.4 EXERCISE 8

Agent	Good morning Towers Car Insurance. How can I help you?
Client	Hello. I was wondering if you could give me a quote for my car, please. I'd like to insure it for a period of 12 months.
Agent	Certainly. I need to take down a few details first of all. Can I have your name please?
Client	Certainly. It's James Bartolo.
Agent	Sorry can you say that again please?
Client	Sure. James Bartolo. That's B-A-R-T-O-L-O.
Agent	Okay, thanks, and your date of birth?
Client	It's the first of the eighth 1973.
Agent	Great and can you give me your address please?
Client	Sure, it's 146 Eastern Rd, Chester.
Agent	Fabulous. Now is the insurance for just yourself?
Client	No, actually my wife drives the car, too. Her name is Alice Jackson and her date of birth is the twenty-third of the fourth 1968.
Agent	That's OK, I just need to write Yes or No. And the make and model of the car you wish to insure.
Client	It's a 1998 Ford Laser.
Agent	OK. And do you have any idea of the value of the car?
Client	Yes it's around £4000. I only bought it about a week ago.
Agent	Okay and do either you or your wife have any previous convictions or disqualifications? I'm sorry we have to ask this question but of course it affects the price of the insurance cover.
Client	Not a problem. No, actually we both have clean driving licences … nothing so far, touch wood!
Agent	Good, so I can write NONE for that question. Now who were you previously insured with?
Client	With Aitken Insurance.
Agent	I'm sorry, could you spell that?

Client	Yes, it's A-I-T-K-E-N. I actually have a three years' no claims bonus, too.
Agent	Great, that will bring the price down a little for you, too. Okay, if you just give me a few minutes, I'll work out a price for you now. That looks like it will be £275 per year.
Client	That sounds good to me. Can I pay for that now over the telephone? (fade out)

Listening **1.10**   EXERCISE   **1**

Agent	Hello. Sydney Tourist Information. How can I help you?
Tourist	Hello. I'm ringing from the UK. I'm coming over soon for a few months. I'm going to be in Sydney for the first few weeks and I was wondering if you could give me some information on what to do, where to go and what to see.
Agent	Certainly. Can you tell me when you're coming and I'll look at our special events calendar.
Tourist	Yes, I'm coming in the last week of January.
Agent	Well, you're in luck. If you're interested, you will be able to see the annual Sydney Mardi Gras.
Tourist	Oh yes, my friend told me about that. When does it actually start?
Agent	Well, it starts in late January and continues into February. The whole event lasts three weeks. It incorporates exhibitions, music, plays, art and literature, and ends in a parade and a big street party. Over one million people come, and the final night party is often sold out well in advance, so you should book if you want to go to any nightclubs or even get a hotel room near the area.
Tourist	Where can I get any more information?
Agent	Well, they have a website with all the details, so you'd probably be best starting there. Is there anything else I can tell you?
Tourist	No, that's fine for now. Thanks very much.
Agent	No problem. Goodbye.
Tourist	Bye.

Listening **1.10**   EXERCISE   **4**

A major problem faced by people in South America is the uneven distribution of the key areas where people choose to live. To be more precise, I'm referring to the problem of overpopulation. The cities are extremely overpopulated and it is here that it is very difficult to provide basic services. Mexico City is home to 20 million people – that's 25% of the total Mexican population living on only 2% of the national territory. The negative effect of such rapid urbanisation, as experienced by other developing countries, is the huge and devastating increase in urban poverty. With so many people living in such close proximity, the situation is becoming increasingly desperate as a result of poor sanitation, which is leading to serious health issues.

Environmental protection groups are concerned about this situation, not only for the well-being of people, but also because of the effect of urban poverty on the environment. Experts argue that in the presence of poverty, environmental destruction is inevitable, due to lack of resources to prevent it, and lack of education or awareness of the problems caused to the environment amongst the country's people. Critics claim that the Mexican government has done very little to increase the general public's awareness of the dangers of inadequate waste disposal and what both individuals and the government can do to improve the situation.

An additional problem is that, in Mexico, electricity demand exceeds the supply capabilities and the country does not have the necessary monetary investment available to improve its electricity supply standards to those required.

Energy saving and education regarding energy saving is a key to improving the situation in Mexico today. Steps to achieve this have already begun: in 1989 The National Commission of Energy Saving was established in order to educate the general population of the implications of overuse of power and the benefits of cutting down.

To summarise the first section of this talk, the environmental issues faced by Mexico at present can be attributed to three main areas of concern. The first is growth in population, the second is urban concentration of that population and the third is the related per capita demand of natural resources and energy which cannot be matched. With a problem of this scale, the people should not be turning so much to the Mexican government, but should be looking for an answer in the international community, as I will explain after the break.

Listening 1.10   REVIEW

S	Hello, I wonder if you could help me. I am interested in enrolling in your MBA programme. Could you give me some information please?
R	Yes, of course. I'll take a few details first of all and I'll give you a copy of our prospectus.
S	Oh that's okay. I already have one here. I've been researching the MBA courses in the local area, so I already have lots of course information!
R	That's great. Okay, so first of all, can you tell me your name please?
S	Yes, of course. It's Anne Hawberry.
R	Hawberry. Is that H-A-W-B-E-R-R-Y?
S	Yes, that's right.
R	Okay, and what's your date of birth, Ms Hawberry?
S	The 22nd of May, 1981.
R	That's great. And were you born in the UK?
S	Yes, I was.
R	All right, can you give me some contact details please?
S	Sure. My address is 26 Simon Place in Brighton and my telephone number is 01903 714 721.
R	Sorry, can you tell me your contact number once again?
S	Yes, it's 01903 714 721.
R	Okay. Great. And do you have a mobile phone number?
S	No, I don't – is it important?
R	No that's OK, I'll just write it on your form – no … mobile … phone. Now just a few additional questions. Are you working or studying anywhere else at the moment?
S	Yes. I am working for Lloyd Enterprise in the city as a secretary and I am also attending a computer course part-time in the evenings.
R	Great. So can you give me some details about your educational background? We need to make sure that your qualifications match the entry requirements.
S	Yes, I completed a Business degree a year ago. I've been working since my graduation, but the job market is very competitive these days, so I'd like to do some postgraduate study now.
R	Okay that sounds fine. Your degree is relevant and it is good that you have some work experience, too. I do need to warn you though that our MBA programme is extremely popular and gets full quickly, so would you be interested in applying for any alternative courses if your application is not successful this time?
S	Well … My first choice would of course be the MBA, but yes, I've had a good look through your prospectus and I would also be interested in the International Marketing course.
R	That's great, it's always a good idea to keep your options open just in case.
R	Finally, can you tell me where you learned about our courses here?
S	Actually my cousin studied the MBA course two years ago and she recommended it to me.

R   Okay, well thank you for coming in today. I will pass your details on to our admissions department. They should contact you this week with a formal application form and they usually invite MBA candidates to come in for an interview.

S   Okay, well thanks for your time.

R   No problem. Good luck with your application.

Listening 2.4   EXERCISE 3

R   Hello, City Council. How can I help you?

C   Oh hello. I'm interested in starting a part-time evening class and I understand that there is a new scheme being run by the council. Could you tell me a little more about it please?

R   Yes, certainly. You are right, we are just starting some brand-new 10-week evening courses especially for adults. Enrolment closes next week for next term so you are just in time. We have information leaflets here, so if you tell me what type of course you are interested in, I can put some in the post for you.

C   That would be great. But you know I'm not all that sure about what I want to study. It's been a long time now since I left school and I haven't studied anything since. I've been at home, you know, looking after my family. But the children have started school now, so I am very keen to get some training and look for a part-time job. Can you give me an idea as to what course might be the most useful for me?

R   Okay. Well, we have lots of courses on offer. We have the traditional school subjects of English literature, English language, mathematics, etc. – these are for people who may have forgotten the basics, if they left school a long time ago. We also have new subjects which older people may never have studied before such as word-processing, spreadsheets and even web design and computer programming. It really depends on what skills you already have and how far you want to go as to which course would be best.

C   I see ... well, I've always wanted to learn something about computers. Do you have beginner classes?

R   Yes, no problem at all. We used to have classes of up to 10 people, but for our new courses we guarantee that there will be no more than eight people in the class, so you are assured of lots of attention from the teacher. We are going to create different level classes so you can feel comfortable and work at your own speed. You can sign up for two or three classes if you want to. You know, choose classes that would complement each other, so if you are interested in computers you might want to sign up for the word processing, spreadsheets and maths classes this time, then maybe advanced word processing and desktop publishing next time, it's up to you. The good thing about the courses is that you will receive a national certificate for each course you complete. It will certainly help you if you are going on to look for work afterwards.

C   I'd be really interested in signing up for more than one course, but I'm a bit concerned about the cost. How much are the courses?

R   Well they are council run, so the courses are subsidised. What you pay actually depends on how much you earn. If your income is high then you will have to pay the full amount, but the courses are free for unemployed people. It is best for you to make an appointment to see the course organiser and he will be able to help you decide which courses to do and work out how much they will cost.

C   Okay. When should I come in?

R   I'll give you the course leader's number. Ring him direct and make an appointment. His name is Mike Edwards and his direct line is 263 8147. Oh, and remember that the courses are not here in the council offices. We are running them all in the town hall. It has great rooms for study and a refreshment area too. It's easy to find, just straight across from the council building here.

Listening **2.4** REVIEW

I'd like to talk about the changes to our leisure time, and I'll start by talking about lifestyle changes over recent years for women. As we all know, the wife and mother of the family has traditionally been responsible for organising and completing household tasks for the family. However, particularly over the last decade or so, we have seen a greater number of women continuing to work after marriage and returning to work after having children. This has significantly reduced the amount of time available for household chores. The result is that nowadays, the majority of people own and regularly use products such as dishwashers or microwaves. The modern family often considers hours spent on cleaning and cooking as a waste of valuable time and generally we are all interested in finding ways of reducing the number of hours we need to devote to such tasks.

While washing machines have long been thought of as necessities by families, nowadays, so too are microwaves and dishwashers. These goods can drastically reduce the amount of time we need to spend running our home and increase the amount of time available not only to go to work, but also to spend on leisure pursuits.

As society develops and we become richer, we put more value on our leisure time and our possessions. The richer a society, the more demanding it becomes. People are no longer happy to work long hours for little return. Expensive holidays, expensive clothes and cars all become more important the more materialistic the society in which we live. Acquiring 'things' and joining the 'race of acquisition' means that modern society spends a lot of time and money purchasing unnecessary goods. Although expensive and persuasive marketing techniques are partly responsible, the demand for such goods often comes from young professionals, those with the money to endlessly upgrade things simply because a better model is made available.

Our obsession with the newest and best products available, while good for the economy, can also have a negative impact on the environment. It is not appropriate to over-produce appliances and over-use electricity to keep these unnecessary appliances operating in our homes. We often forget about the damage we have done to, and continue to do to, the environment.

Others opposed to the overuse of appliances and technology also argue that from a social point of view, over-reliance on gadgets means that people are losing the ability to be creative. Traditionally it was considered an enviable skill to prepare meals night after night for our families. Nowadays, women are more likely to gain approval from others for their success in their careers than their ability in the kitchen. Along with microwaves have come ready-cooked meals, pre-washed vegetables and our reliance on take-away food when we are too busy to cook it ourselves.

While there are obvious advantages and disadvantages to our increasingly active buying behaviour and changing wants and desires, it is likely that our desire to purchase labour-saving items will continue, so it is therefore inevitable that production of such goods will increase. We can only hope to educate ourselves and our children to buy goods we need, not just goods that are available, and we must also consider their environmental impact. In short, moderation is the most important word for the future.

I thank you very much for coming today and listening … (fade out)

Listening 2.10   EXERCISE 4

Dialogue in a rental agency

Emiliano	Hello my name is Emiliano. I am a student here and I would like to rent a house for six months. (Q1)
Rental agent	Okay, well you have come to the right place! We specialise in short-term rental. First of all I would like to get a few details from you. Can you give me your full name please?
Emiliano	Yes. It is Emiliano Nespola.
Rental agent	And can you tell me your present address please?
Emiliano	Yes. It's 17 Meadow Way, Penrose. I'm living with a homestay family at the moment.
Rental agent	That's great! Now do you have any identification with you? Oh, and we will need a reference from someone who knows you here. Maybe your homestay family?
Emiliano	Yes, okay. Here's my passport and the card from my language school (Q2). My referee can be Mrs Alice Thompson, she's my homestay mother and she won't mind, I'm sure. You can contact her at the same address as me of course.
Rental agent	Okay. If we need to contact you, should we leave a message with your homestay?
Emiliano	No, you can speak to me directly. My cellphone number is 021 548 3534. (Q3)
Rental agent	Great. Now, do you have a bank account? You will need to pay your rent by direct debit – you know, it will come out of your account automatically every month.
Emiliano	Okay. I don't have my bank account details with me now but I can get them and bring them back later today.
Rental agent	That's fine. Now can you tell me what kind of house you are looking for? Do you want to rent by yourself?
Emiliano	No. I'm looking for a three-bedroom house … I want to rent with my two friends. I'll bring them in to see you later today.
Rental agent	Okay. And what areas are you interested in renting in?
Emiliano	Well, here's a map. Can you see my school? I don't have a car so I need to take some kind of public transport to school and I don't want to travel for more than 30 minutes each way. (Q4) Do you think you have anything which is suitable?
Rental agent	Yes we do. Here is a list of available properties. I'll highlight the ones that could be of interest to you. Look at the map and go and have a look at the houses with your friends. Do you have a friend with a car?
Emiliano	Yes I do.
Rental agent	Good. So go and look outside the houses, it will give you an idea of what the area is like, but remember don't go into the garden or knock on the door. If you want to go in and have a look, let me know and we can arrange an appointment.
Emiliano	Okay. Can you give me an idea of price?
Rental agent	Yes. If you look at the list, you can see the weekly rent written next to the house address. (Q5)
Emiliano	Oh yes, I can see it now. Do I need to pay anything else?
Rental agent	Yes, you need to pay a deposit which you will get back when you move out (Q6) and you have to pay a non-refundable agent fee which is equivalent to one week's rent. You will have to pay your bills when they come in every month too, of course.
Emiliano	Okay, well thank you very much for your help. What time should I come back with my friends and my bank details?
Rental agent	How about 2.30 this afternoon?
Emiliano	That sounds good. Thank you for your help. I'll see you later.
Rental agent	Thanks for coming in. Goodbye.

Listening **2.10** EXERCISE 6

Given the general standard of living in New Zealand, many people are surprised by the decline in the level of home ownership. Over the last 15 years the number of homeowners has fallen by over 7%, yet this is not a reflection of financial pressures. House prices in New Zealand are relatively stable, so there is no need to worry about a house losing value, and few people are dissuaded by the cost of maintenance on the building itself. The reason for the increasing popularity of renting is in fact the result of fluidity in the job market, and the fact that obligations involved in a house often tie people to specific locations which do not support this lifestyle.

Listening **2.10** EXERCISE 9 REVIEW

Thank you very much for inviting me here today. I understand that you all own your own home, and some of you may be interested in buying additional property here in the city, so I hope you will find the information I am going to share with you useful and informative. I am going to talk about the situation with property here in the city. The city centre of any area is obviously going to have the highest prices and as more and more people are competing for houses in this area, both renting and buying are becoming increasingly difficult.

It is most people's dream to, one day, own their own house. House ownership gives us a feeling of having achieved something and we can see clearly what we have worked so hard for all our lives. It can give us a sense of security for our old age and a knowledge that we will hopefully have something to pass on to our children. However, buying a house, particularly for first-time buyers, is becoming more and more difficult, not only due to increasing prices but also because of the need for a substantial deposit. For younger people, buying their first home is very difficult and often impossible. Young couples who cannot get the deposit together, need to rent for a long time and sometimes forever.

While, traditionally, homes near the centre of the city have been the most desirable, people are now looking further afield. This has happened for a number of reasons, the main one being that our style of work is changing along with that of other countries such as the USA. In certain professions, for example sales and computing, it is no longer necessary for people to be based in an office full-time. More and more people are beginning to work from home which means they can avoid the hustle and bustle of rush-hour traffic jams into work and have more freedom to choose to live in a more rural and peaceful location.

My company deals with finding property for both purchasers and renters in the city area. One of my main roles within the company is to find investment properties for people who wish to plan ahead for their future.

(short pause)

An investment property is usually at the cheaper end of the market. People buy investment properties, not to live in, but in addition to their own home in order to rent it out to other people.

The advantage of putting your savings into property for the future is that you can be pretty certain that, as a long-term investment, your money will safely increase in value in line with inflation. Many people are turning to property investment instead of pension schemes as we hear the horror stories of countries such as the UK, where people have invested all their lives into their pension schemes to find that now their money is relatively worthless.

Houses automatically earn what is known as capital gains; that is, for every year you own the property, it becomes more valuable and often gives a better rate of interest on your money than most banks do. However, that is not to say there are no risks. There are people who buy property when the market is high and prices are inflated beyond their true value, only to find that when the housing market slows down, they are in a state of negative equity. Negative equity is a situation that arises when you owe more for the house than the house itself is worth.

In short, the best advice is to be aware of the ups and downs of the housing market. Property investment, if handled correctly, can be enormously satisfying.

I hope that this has given you an insight into the basics of the property market. Thank you for listening. Please raise your hand if you have any questions and I will try to be of assistance.

Listening 3.4 EXERCISE 4

1 There are 13 National parks in New Zealand.

2 There are 27% more men than women in Korea.

3 The King cobra's venom can kill 20 people.

4 The universe is composed of 90% hydrogen.

5 The movie *Titanic* made $1 billion.

6 Three million works of art are in an art gallery in St Petersburg.

Listening 3.4 EXERCISE 6

1 World War II ended on the 11th of November, 1945.

2 Princess Diana died on August 30th 1997.

3 On September 11th 2001 the Twin Towers in America were attacked.

4 England won the World Cup on the 30th of July 1966.

5 President John F. Kennedy was assassinated in November 1963, on the 22nd I think.

6   The *Titanic* sank on April the 14th, 1912.

Listening 3.10 EXERCISE 3

Mary	Hey – don't throw that can away!
Sam	Why not? I've finished with it.
Mary	Yes, but you can recycle things like that.
Sam	Oh, I haven't got time to recycle everything I throw away.
Mary	That's a terrible attitude! Don't you care about …?
John	Hello, you two.
Sam	Hi, John
John	What are you arguing about?
Mary	Oh, Sam says he doesn't have time to recycle. What do you think?
John	Well, I agree that it can be difficult sometimes. Do you always recycle everything then, Mary?

Mary	Yes. I think everyone should. I mean, look at the state of the planet. If we don't all start making an effort now, it could be too late.
John	Well, one of the reasons I don't recycle as often as I should is that I don't really know where to go. There are no recycling facilities near me.
Sam	Well, I know I said I haven't got time, but actually, there is a bottle bank near the supermarket just up the road, so I suppose there are limited local facilities.
John	So you can do your recycling outside the supermarket?
Sam	Yes, but like I said, only limited – it's only a bottle bank.
Mary	Well, I don't have a car, so it's very difficult for me, but I still do it. Sometimes a friend comes over and we take our recycling together, but not very often, so if your facilities are limited, then mine are very limited.
Sam	Well, I suppose if you go to all that trouble I might make more of an effort.
Mary	Good. If it was up to me, I'd encourage more people to recycle.
Sam	How?
Mary	Well, how about some kind of incentive, a reward for anyone who makes an effort to recycle.
John	That's a good idea, but if you think everyone should recycle, then why not penalise those who don't recycle instead of giving something to people that do. If there was a fine for anyone caught throwing recyclable materials in the rubbish, people would take more notice.
Sam	Well, now you're going too far. Do you really want anyone going through your rubbish just to check if you're following the rules? No, I don't think fines are a good idea.
Mary	Well, I think we should be doing something. Anyway, I have to go. I've got my social science class next. See you later.
John	Yeah, see you later.
Sam	Bye.

Listening 3.10 REVIEW

Interviewer	Thank you very much for tuning in today to listen to our weekly hour on conservation issues. Last week we spoke about the impact of environmental changes on primates, and this week to continue the theme we have invited in a specialist by the name of Professor Andrew Ripley, all the way from USA, to tell us more about the problems faced by the cat family. Professor Ripley, thank you very much for joining us today.
Prof Ripley	It's my pleasure, thank you very much for inviting me.
Interviewer	So I understand that you spent a great proportion of your time travelling the globe and monitoring changes in population levels of the cat family.
Prof Ripley	Yes, that's correct. Of course we are not talking about the domestic cat here, but their majestic cousins such as the lion, tiger and jaguar to name but a few.
Interviewer	Which member of the cat family do you yourself find to be the most fascinating?
Prof Ripley	Well, I've spent a lot of time recently studying jaguars, but the lion is still my personal favourite. It is the world's most social cat and unusual in the way in which it chooses to group together with others of its species. Prides of lions basking in the sunshine are probably one of people's most vivid perceptions of the African bush.
Interviewer	Yes certainly … I totally agree with you. Can you tell me the current lion population in Africa these days?
Prof Ripley	Well … it is very difficult to measure it accurately. Figures range from 100 000, to as few as 30 000, but it is generally estimated that there are 50 000. In order to

	maintain the population and protect the species from poachers, many are moved to protected areas.
Interviewer	Which member of the cat family do you feel is most at risk?
Prof Ripley	For different reasons, a number of species of the cat family are endangered. Sometimes due to natural predators or environmental changes, but mainly because of the threat of hunters. For example, I am sure you are aware, the bones and body parts of tigers have been, and still are, traditionally used in medicines in the Far East. Because of this and the demand for medicine made from tiger parts, their numbers have been falling for some time and to date there are fewer than 6000 tigers living in their natural habitat of the forests and plains of Asia.
Interviewer	What is being done to curb the population decrease?
Prof Ripley	Well, specialists such as myself work closely with conservationist groups such as the World Wildlife Federation, or WWF, to protect tigers from illegal hunting. WWF considers the drop in tiger numbers to be catastrophic and they are working hard to conserve the populations in China, India, Indonesia, Malaysia, Thailand, Vietnam and Russia.
Interviewer	I understand that poaching is not the only problem faced by the leopard… let me get this right … is it the snow leopard which lives in the mountains in Asia?
Prof Ripley	Yes, it is. Poaching has been a problem, but not the most important. Its natural prey – the animals it hunts – is declining too. Its natural habitat in high-altitude areas, specifically the pastures, is threatened by the growth of agriculture. It is this that is causing the main problem for the snow leopard. It is going to be extremely difficult for numbers to recover, but again the WWF has been working hard to continue to fund projects to aid the snow leopard in Nepal and Pakistan, and hopefully Bhutan very soon.
Interviewer	Well this is fascinating information you are giving us, Professor, we are just going into a short commercial break. When we come back I have a few questions for you about the puma and the jaguar. Remember listeners, there will be an opportunity to phone in and voice any opinions or questions you may have for the professor in ten minutes.

Listening 4.4 EXERCISE 1

In 1946, the United Nations established an agency that was designed to encourage nations to share ideas in education, science, culture and communication, and that was how UNESCO was first formed. UNESCO stands for the United Nations Educational, Scientific and Cultural Organization. More than 180 nations belong to UNESCO. With headquarters in France and over 60 offices worldwide, the agency is involved in a number of projects including international science programmes and regional and cultural history projects, as well as agreements to secure the world's cultural and natural heritage. It is this last point that resulted in the UNESCO Universal Declaration on Cultural Diversity, which was adopted by all of the Member States at a General Conference in 2001.

Listening **4.4** EXERCISE 2

Paul	Hey, do you know any important dates?
Gail	What do you mean?
Paul	Well, I'm writing a report on some famous festivals or significant world events and I can't think of any more.
Gail	Hmmm, what have you got already?
Paul	The only ones I can think of are Bastille Day on the 14th of July and Elvis's death on the 16th of August.
Gail	OK. What about the 25th of January? You know Burns' Night – for that famous Scottish poet. Oh, and the 4th of April – that was the day Martin Luther King was assassinated.
Paul	Who?
Gail	You know, Martin Luther King. And then there's ANZAC Day. That's on the 24th, no sorry, the 25th of April. Do you need anymore?
Paul	No, that's great. Thanks!
Gail	No problem.

Listening **4.4** EXERCISE 3

Hi. My name is Adrian Wolffe. That's spelt W-O-L-F-F-E. I work for a research company based in North America, but I'm originally from Lllangollen – that's L-L-A-N-G-O-L-L-E-N. Now I have been asked to talk to you all today about some of my research regarding the Navajo Indians. Can I just spell that for you – it's N-A-V-A-J-O. This Indian tribe is particularly famous for its contribution during the Second World War, when secret code was sent using the Navajo language of Athapaksan. Perhaps I should also spell that for you. It's A-T-H-A-P-A-K-S-A-N.

Listening **4.4** EXERCISE 4

Hello. I'd like to talk to you today on the subject of cultural heritage. Now, looking around this room, I see that there are a number of different nationalities, so there are a number of slightly different opinions as to what 'cultural heritage' actually means. However, for the subject of this lecture, I would like to talk in general about those features of a culture or a community that have been passed down through the generations.

Although it is true that some people do not fully appreciate their cultural heritage, the majority of people are fully aware of their background. I would also argue that many young people in fact do see the value in many traditions. The belief that they reject them is a misconception; they, like every generation before them, have simply adapted the traditions of their parents to suit modern conditions. Most traditional cultures will almost certainly not disappear, but they may change as they are passed down through the generations.

Listening **4.4** EXERCISE 5

In our top story tonight, billionaire businessman Richard Pease has been given 28 days to show the courts records of all financial dealings. His company, Macrovisual, has been accused of tax evasion. If found guilty, Pease faces a fine of up to 4.5 million pounds and up to 18 months in jail.

Petrol prices are due to rise another 4p a litre from next week. In response to criticism, the government claims that this is due to increased transportation costs. It is the fourth rise in petrol in the last 12 months.

And in other news, Stoke City have secured their third straight victory of the season, beating Port Vale 3–0. Port Vale have yet to win a match this season.

Listening **4.10** EXERCISE 2

Starting at the beginning, you can see the on-off switch just beneath the two lights. Having turned the machine on, these lights now become very important. When the light on the left has gone out, you can begin making coffee as it means the water is now hot enough. Next to that is the water level light. If this is illuminated, it means the machine does not have enough water. It is essential that you turn the machine off and add more water the moment this light comes on, otherwise you could damage the heating element. Once you have checked that both the heater light and the water level light are off, make sure the filter holder – that's the part with the handle, just under the control panel – is in place. Once you have your cups ready, it is time to press the coffee delivery switch – that's the button just above the filter holder beside the boiler meter. Remember to take a quick look at the meter as it tells you the exact temperature of the water.

On both the left- and right-hand side of the machine, on the same level as the filter holder, you can see the steam pipes used for heating milk. These steam taps need to be cleaned regularly to avoid blocking.

And finally, if you do spill any coffee, don't worry. Just make sure that the drainage pipe at the bottom of the machine is leading into a sink or a suitable waste container. As with the steam taps, the drainage pipe needs regular cleaning.

Listening **4.10** EXERCISE 5

Jenny	Hi John. Are you nearly ready?
John	Oh … no. I don't think I'm going to make it tonight.
Jenny	Why?
John	I've got this assignment to finish for tomorrow.
Jenny	Well, maybe I can help. What do you have to do?
John	I have to do a short presentation on some household object, and I just can't think of anything. I have to talk about what it is and the parts in it.
Jenny	Well, why not make it simple? Why not describe a bottle or a can?
John	That's far too simple!
Jenny	OK, how about an aerosol can?
John	Mmm … maybe. What labels can you put on it?
Jenny	First you'd have to draw an aerosol can. First thing you could label would be the hairspray or whatever was in the can. You'd just label that 'product' I suppose. Then you'd have to label the area above the product as the propellant.
John	Is that the gas that presses down on the contents of the can, forcing it out through the dip tube?
Jenny	Yes, you've got it!
John	OK, so far so good. Now, at the top of the aerosol there are quite a few things to label, so I would have to write quite small.
Jenny	Unless you drew a couple of lines and showed an enlarged picture of that area.
John	Yes, that would work. Then I could start labelling from the top to the bottom.

Jenny	The first thing on the enlargement would be the nozzle.
John	The what?
Jenny	The nozzle. You know, N-O-Z-Z-L-E. Then the seal.
John	Right. Then all I'd need is the spring.
Jenny	No, you'd need to label the inlet first, then the final part would be the spring. Anyway, that's it. You've finished! We can go out now.
John	Well, I have to type all that into the computer first, and draw the can.
Jenny	Awww …

Listening **5.4**   EXERCISE **2**

Well, continuing our series of lectures on occupational health issues, I'd like to talk to you today about a condition which is particularly relevant in these days of computers – repetitive strain injury, or RSI. RSI results from repeated physical movements which end up doing damage to tendons, nerves and muscles. The increasing importance of computers in the workplace, and the number of people who spend each and every day in front of one, has resulted in a dramatic rise in injuries to the hands, arms, and shoulders. Not only typing, but also the use of the simple computer mouse is having a detrimental effect, as long periods of repeated movement slowly wear and damage the body.

This is not a new injury in the workplace, nor is it entirely the fault of technology. Anyone repeating the same pattern of limited physical movements is likely to experience a degree of RSI. The situation is inevitably made worse if those who feel its effects do not take regular breaks or reconsider their body position. In cases of typing-related RSI, the cause can often be found in poor posture or typing at an angle or sitting too low in the chair, forcing arms into an unnatural position for the best part of eight hours a day.

One way to prevent a serious case of RSI, one that could see you unable to work for some weeks or even months, is to recognise the early signs. There are a number of typical signs, such as tightness, discomfort, stiffness, soreness or burning in the hands, wrists, fingers, forearms or elbows. This often leads to a feeling of coldness or numbness in the hands. Pain in the upper back, shoulders or neck can also suggest that some time away from the computer is needed. Ignoring these signs can lead to severe damage, in which sufferers are woken at night with the pain, or the symptoms can be felt within moments of typing.

As I said earlier, posture is essential in order to minimise the likelihood of RSI, and good typing habits and good-quality equipment can also help. However, the most important way of avoiding RSI is simple and cheap – take a break. By taking short, regular breaks, and exercising the muscles in the hands, arms and shoulders, the tension that causes RSI can be relieved.

Moving on, I'd like now to talk about another form of RSI. When sitting at a keyboard for extended periods, it is not only your arms that suffer, but also your eyes. Many people sit far too close to their monitor, and this leads to a number of other symptoms, particularly headaches and blurred vision. However, this form of RSI is relatively simple to overcome. By increasing the font size; that is, the size of the letters you are typing, there is less need to sit so close to the monitor. Another thing that can be done is to change the colours, especially the bright white background common on most word-processing software. A softer tone, such as a light grey, is much easier on the eyes and is considerably less likely to lead to any kind of repetitive strain.

Now, before I finish, I would like to add a personal opinion to the subject. Earlier I told you of one way to avoid serious damage as a result of RSI, but no matter what steps you take, how you sit or how many exercises you do, the best way to avoid any computer-related strain is to use it less. There are times when a simple pen and paper are just as effective as the fastest computer. Taking every opportunity to find an alternative way of completing daily tasks not only reduces the damage done, but also gives the weakened areas of the body time to heal.

Well, that concludes this section of the lecture. We'll take a short break before continuing the lecture on occupational health and safety, looking specifically at the government's role.

Listening 5.4 EXERCISE 5

Interviewer	I'm here today with Helen Warner, who has been a vegetarian for many years and is going to talk a little about vegetarianism. Helen, the concept of vegetarianism seems to have interested a number of our listeners, who have sent in some questions. To begin, what made you want to become a vegetarian?
Helen	Well, when I was 16, I had friends who were vegetarian and they introduced me to the idea. My parents were typical of their generation, and ate meat at least three or four times a week, so I didn't really think about it too much until a few years later. It was while I was at university that I really thought about it, and decided that it was unfair to eat meat when there are so many alternatives available.
Interviewer	Is there anything you miss about not eating meat?
Helen	Ummm. No, not really. As I said, there are so many substitutes available these days, perhaps the most important of which comes from the soya bean. Soya is so versatile, and is the staple substitute for most vegetarians.
Interviewer	So what about the nutritional value of vegetarian food? Isn't it true that there are some vitamins that you can't get from soya or vegetables alone? Surely people need these vitamins?
Helen	Yes, that's correct. But actually there is only one vital vitamin that is only present in meat – that's vitamin B12. Most vegetarians are aware of the implication of this and actually take B12 supplement in the form of tablets. Of course the way you cook vegetables is also very important in preserving vitamins. Many countries, particularly the UK, have a reputation for overcooking vegetables. Water-soluble vitamins – you know, where the vitamins are dissolved into the water – are often lost. Vitamin C is a common example. However, this loss of vitamins can be avoided by microwaving or steaming vegetables, which is what I do whenever I cook. Some people don't want to change their cooking habits too much, so if you do boil them, simply cut down on the cooking time.
Interviewer	So a vegetarian diet is fairly healthy then?
Helen	Oh yes. A lot of people believe that vegetarianism is unhealthy, but that's not actually the case. Vegetarians are actually considerably healthier than many meat eaters. Consider for a minute the health aspects of the incredible amount of meat this country and others like it consume. The statistics for beef eating, for example, are quite frightening. The world figure for beef consumption is slightly less than 11 kg per person each year. Yet in Europe, the average consumption is nearly double that at 21 kilos per person, and in the USA it is even worse, with the average person eating 44 kg of beef every year.
Interviewer	So are you suggesting that people stop eating meat altogether and everyone adopts a vegetarian lifestyle?
Helen	No, not at all. Even in the healthiest diets there is still a place for meat, but it should be eaten in moderation. Many nutritionists think of foods in terms of a pyramid, with the foods we can eat relatively freely at the bottom and the foods we should carefully restrict at the top. The majority of our diet should be composed of cereals, which would go on the bottom row of the pyramid. In this category could also be included such things as rice and pasta. Next, a good diet is followed by a roughly equal amount of vegetables and fruit. I have at least two servings a day of fruit and

vegetables whenever possible. In decreasing quantities, you can then eat dairy foods – eggs, cheese, etc. Almost at the top of the food pyramid comes fish – carefully prepared of course, not dripping in oil or batter! – and white meat. Chicken, for example, is a comparatively healthy meat, but again, a lot of this comes down to preparation methods. Right at the top of the pyramid come the ingredients of far too many western meals – red meat and potatoes. It is particularly in that area that I would suggest moderation.

Interviewer   Well, thank you very much Helen. I'm sure that a lot of listeners are interested in your views. How could they find out more about the health benefits of vegetarian options?

Helen   Well there are lots of websites and books on healthy eating and vegetarianism, but it is always important to remember to consult your doctor before making any radical changes to your diet or lifestyle.

Listening 5.10   EXERCISE 3

Amongst increasing social and political pressure to quit, there is finally some good news for smokers. Research presented to the European Society of Cardiology states that there are sufficient beneficial chemicals in two glasses of red wine to suspend the harmful effect that smoking one cigarette has on the functioning of arteries.

Of course, the findings do not suggest that drinking red wine allows you to smoke as much as you like, and it is still a long way from finding any kind of drug that is capable of reversing the harmful effects of long-term smoking.

The health effects connected with red wine are not really new. The Romans and the Greeks considered it as a form of medicine, possibly because of the abundance of polyphenols, naturally occurring chemicals which have a cleansing effect on the arteries.

Listening 5.10   EXERCISE 4

First and most importantly, I'll tell you where you should go from tomorrow for your lectures and classes. The Health Sciences building is on the west side of the campus, opposite the library, beside the history department. As you are probably aware, there are six modules to the course, which will take a year to complete. That's two modules each term. In the first module of this term, you will be looking at current laws with regard to health and safety in the workplace. Don't forget that as you progress through the course, you should be building your thesis. This will need to be completed by the end of the year. Coursework will also be credited to your final grade, but the most important part of the course is the thesis. Now, the final thing I want to tell you, and again you should know this, is that there will be a number of guest speakers throughout your course. They will come from a number of different medical backgrounds, but they will all be giving you their views on the relevance of health sciences in their occupations.

Listening 5.10   REVIEW

Interviewer   Over the past 50 years, there have been some radical changes in medicine as it is known in the west. This is largely the result of vast improvements in technology, but also in the rising importance of 'alternative' treatments. I have with me today Matthew East, a registered osteopath and a supporter of alternative techniques in healthcare. Matthew, can you tell us more about osteopathy?

Matthew East	Well, perhaps the first thing I should say is that the term 'alternative' is actually a little misleading, as I am referring to approaches and attitudes to health that were in common use long before western medicine was established. I prefer the term 'natural'. Anyway, I'll begin by telling you a little about osteopathy. Basically, osteopathy is the manipulation of muscles in order to alleviate stresses and tensions that lead to pain. Now, unlike western medicine, osteopathy considers the whole body, not just the affected area, and this is a very important principle of natural remedies. The whole body must be considered before a course of treatment can be decided upon. You see, the aim of therapies like osteopathy is not only to repair the body, but also to get the body treating itself, and this does not come from treating the symptoms. To give an example, I recently treated a two-month-old baby who was screaming all day and was even worse at night. The couple had taken the baby to their doctor, but the only advice they were given was that the baby 'would grow out of it'. However, the real problem stemmed from a difficult birth which put pressure on their baby's neck. After ten minutes of gentle manipulation the pressure was released and within 20 minutes, the baby was quiet and calm for the first time. This was achieved without drugs or operations. Avoiding such invasive methods of treatment highlights another of the differences between western medicine and a more natural approach. You see, western medicine often uses surgery in order to find a solution to problems that could have been addressed with simple remedies. A medical approach that looks closely at how essential an operation is before it is performed would offer patients a considerably less stressful method of treatment, not to mention the financial savings. Natural remedies actually amount to about ten per cent of the cost of a western course of treatment.

I'd like to mention the subject of surgery again a little later, but I would like to say at this point that there are those that claim that the benefits of osteopathy and herbal therapies are largely psychological, that they have not undergone the clinical trials that pharmaceuticals have. To answer that, you only need to look at the example I gave earlier, of the baby that stopped crying less than an hour after treatment but was obviously far too young to react because of purely psychological factors. Another example can be seen in the successful use of acupuncture in the treatment of animals. In response to criticism regarding clinical trials, it is worth noting that the power of pharmaceutical companies is such that although some drugs fail the standards required of them, they are sometimes still prescribed by doctors.

Moving on to another point, it should be stressed that natural remedies, in addition to having no side effects, can also be applied to any patient. Now I'm not suggesting that the same treatments are used indiscriminately. Although natural remedies can be used with any age group, the treatment selected is very specific to the person. By this I mean that not only the general health of the patient needs to be considered, but also their habits, diet and lifestyle in order to build a complete picture.

However, I am not suggesting that we should reject western medicine entirely. In fact, there have been occasions when I have referred patients to their doctor as I felt that in those cases it was the most suitable course of action. There are many situations in which it is by far the best option. Take emergency surgery, for example. Obviously more natural remedies do not provide the speed required in such cases. The best solution would therefore be an open-minded combination of the two forms. |
| Interviewer | Well, thank you very much, Matthew. That was a very interesting insight into alternative … sorry … natural, treatments. Next week we'll be inviting Dr Moore – that's M-O-O-R-E – onto the programme to argue his case as a doctor. Until next week, then, goodbye. |

Listening **6.4** EXERCISE 2

1 Although an academic education is very important …
2 Having completed this, the next step is …
3 Not only is this essential in the classroom but also …
4 Admittedly, it could be argued that …
5 As a result, many students find themselves …
6 In the same way, Australia has …

Listening **6.4** EXERCISE 5

First, I'd like to thank you all again for coming to this meeting, and to say that I have received apologies from Mrs Brownlow, who won't be able to attend today. Now, I'd like to talk to you about our English language department. As I said in the last meeting, we are looking for some of you to act as mentors for our international students arriving over the coming weeks. Although our college prides itself on having a welcoming environment in which international students can feel at home from the very first day, we know this isn't always so. Feelings of homesickness, isolation and loneliness are somewhat unavoidable, but I would like, as much as possible, to reduce these factors by teaming new students with existing students who have been here some time. To put it another way, I am looking for volunteers to show the new students around, introduce them to people and generally ease them into their studies, so if any of you are willing to help, then please come to my office anytime during the week and let me know. Moving on, I'd also like to talk to you about a temporary teacher who will be joining us for the next week or so. He will be teaching history and sociology, and substituting for Miss Kinsale until her recovery. Talking about that, if anyone wants to send her a card then just let me know by the end of the day as I will be going to the hospital this evening to visit her. Right, unless there is anything else you want to add, we'll close the meeting. I hope to see some of you during the week.

Listening **6.4** EXERCISE 6

1 So from now on, I would like to ask all of you to return library books on time. (Falling intonation indicating end of topic.)
2 You should all read the first chapter of the course book for tomorrow. (Rising intonation indicating that there is more to come.)

Listening **6.4** REVIEW

A: Good afternoon. I'm pleased to see so many of you here today. As I told you all on Monday, the lecture on overpopulation has been postponed until next week as we have a guest speaker today. I'd like to introduce you all to Donald Mackenzie, who has recently returned from a 12-month research project in America. He is here to share with us some of the results of his studies into the problem of illiteracy.

D: Hello. Now, as sociology students, I have no doubt that you are aware that it is commonly believed that one indicator of a developed country is the level of education of its citizens. Most of these nations have free compulsory education for all and strict teacher certification requirements, so it would logically follow that people from countries such as America would be highly educated. Yet this isn't always so: in America alone, 42 million adults cannot read and 50 million can recognise so few printed words they each have the reading ability of a 10-year-old. Frightening statistics indeed, but not as frightening as the trend suggested by current estimates – the number of illiterate adults is increasing by approximately two and a quarter million people each year, and although global statistics have not been compiled, it suggests an extremely disturbing figure.

Inevitably, this is having an impact on employment. In America, the annual cost in welfare programmes and unemployment compensation due to illiteracy stands at six billion US dollars, and an additional $237 billion a year in unrealised earnings is forfeited by people who lack basic reading skills. There is also the cost of post-school literacy programmes, which have been put in place in order to counter this increasing figure. A conservative estimate places the cost of these programmes at 10 billion dollars each year, and growing steadily.

Moving on, I'd like to talk about some of the causes of this increasing illiteracy. Children were taught to read by first learning the alphabet, then the sounds of each letter, how they blended into syllables, and how those syllables made up words. They were taught that English spelling is logical and systematic, and that to become a fluent reader it was necessary to master the alphabetic code in which English words are written, to the point where the code is used automatically with little conscious thought given to it. To make myself clear, I mean readers could sound out the letters, spelling them phonetically. Once a child learned this ability, attention could be turned to more advanced content. It seldom, if ever, occurred to teachers to give children word lists to read, or to make beginner-level readers memorise whole words before learning the components of those words, or to memorise whole stories as today's proponents of the whole-language approach recommend. Several recent studies have found that 90 per cent of remedial reading students in developed countries are not able to decode fluently, accurately, and at an automatic level of response. The currently used 'whole language' method was originally conceived and used in the early 1800s to teach the deaf how to read, a method which has long since been discarded by the teachers of the deaf themselves as inadequate and outmoded.

English is an alphabetic language that, when written, uses letters to represent speech sounds. When students were taught to read, they consciously identified the speech sounds and learned to recognise the letters used to represent them. They were then trained to apply this information to decode the names of written words, understand their meaning, and comprehend the information presented as a complete thought. The English language contains approximately half a million words. Of these words, about 300 compose about three-quarters of the words we use regularly. As I said, in schools where the 'whole language' method is taught, children are constantly memorising sight words during the first three or four grades of school, but are never taught how to unlock the meaning of the other 499 700 or more words.

Whole-language learning causes frustration, poor spelling and hostility towards reading. Very bright children who can't memorise long lists of words and retain their meaning are placed in special education, when all they need is to be taught the 26 letters of the alphabet, the 44 sounds they make, and the 70 common ways to spell those sounds. Some researchers believe dyslexia and the symptoms of Attention Deficit Disorder are actually caused by this reversal of the normal learning sequence.

So why do faulty reading methods continue to be used? Well, in short it's Big Business! The sale of instructional reading programmes is big business today: each year publishing companies compete for the adoption of reading programmes and workbooks which have to be replaced annually. Concentrating on phonics would seriously reduce the cost of education.

Listening **6.10** EXERCISE 2

Joe	Hey, are your parents coming to the graduation ceremony?
Alana	Yes, are yours?
Joe	Well, my mum is but my Dad's away on business.
Alana	Oh, that's a shame.
Joe	I don't mind. It's a bit of a waste of time anyway.
Alana	Aww. You can't say that. It's the end of three years of hard work. It's good to have some kind of occasion.
Joe	I suppose so, but it's going to take all day, and we only have to collect our certificates.
Alana	Yes, but I'm sure you'll want to take photographs of your graduation day.
Joe	Yes, maybe you're right. Have you got your cap and gown yet?
Alana	Well, I have, but it's not very good. I think the tassel…
Joe	Tassel? You mean the cord that comes out of the top and falls down the side of the cap?
Alana	Yes – well, it's quite short. But that's not the problem – I was trying it on a couple of days ago when I found that there was a small mark on it, near the edge.
Joe	Oh no! Can't you fix it?
Alana	I don't think so, but it is right beside the tassel, so I guess I can probably hide it.
Joe	Shame though. Do you have any plans for after the graduation?
Alana	Of course! I'm going to the graduation ball. Aren't you?
Joe	I can't – my mum's taking me back home because I'm … (fade out)

Listening **6.10** REVIEW

Pat	So what was it like in your school then, Lyn?
Lyn	Well, South African schools are very different from schools in Australia. For a start, children don't start their schooling until they are seven – quite a bit later than schools in Australia. What about New Zealand, Gail?
Gail	We're more like Australia. I can't believe children don't go to school until they are seven! When do the parents get any free time?
Lyn	Well, there's still the availability of kindergartens or playschools, it's just that formal education doesn't start until later. I don't think it's such a good idea for children to have to be too academic at such a young age. They should be able to just enjoy themselves.
Pat	Well, yes, but the first school children go to isn't really very academic. It's just an opportunity for children to learn a few basic social skills by playing and learning with other children.
Gail	Yes, I'd agree with that.
Lyn	I guess being so close, Australian and New Zealand schools must be similar then?
Gail	Well, I suppose they do share a lot of similarities, but there're also some differences. For example, children in New Zealand go through intermediate school, but in Australia there's only high school. That's right, isn't it Pat?
Pat	Yes, I think so. What about South Africa, Lyn? Do you have intermediate or high school?
Lyn	Oh, high school.
Pat	Another difference between Australian and New Zealand education is that although both countries have state schools and private schools, our private schools are very often run by religious groups, whereas New Zealand schools are secular.

Gail	That's not true – there are quite a few religious schools in New Zealand.
Pat	Oh, OK. Maybe we are similar.
Lyn	Only a few South African schools have any religious connection, so I guess we're different. Most people go to state schools. Pat, is it true that some people from your country don't have to go to school at all?
Pat	Well, that's partly true. Because of the geography of Australia, there are a lot of children who do not have access to schools, at least on a regular basis. Instead they have a form of correspondence education, where the lessons are actually on the radio and the students send their work in by post. That way they get a lot of what they would if they were in the classroom – apart from the interaction.
Gail	In New Zealand not all students have to go to school either. Some parents have opted for home schooling.
Lyn	Oh, is that like correspondence teaching? We don't really have that.
Gail	Well, we do have correspondence schools but home schooling is different. With home schooling the parents teach the children and set them homework. They have to present a syllabus to their local education authority before they can do that, but it is becoming a more popular choice for some parents. I suppose it also suits parents' own commitments. I mean they don't have to worry about collecting their children from school, and they can always teach over the weekend or in the evening if they want to.
Lyn	Is the school day normally quite long then?
Gail	Not in New Zealand, but I think it can be in Australia.
Pat	Yes, that's right. I think Australia is unusual in that there are extracurricular activities which you have to go to. These are normally sport activities, but there are a few other options.
Lyn	We have activities after school for any student that is interested, but they aren't compulsory. What about in New Zealand, Gail?
Gail	I had to do some sport every week. I didn't really like it, but it was part of the school day so I guess that's not so bad. Anyway, I spent two years at boarding school so things were a little different.
Lyn	Boarding school? What was that like?
Gail	Well, the thing I remember most about it was the strict dress code. There were restrictions on everything! You had to wear a school uniform almost all of the time, and it had to be cleaned and ironed. The length of your skirt had to be no less than one inch above your knees when kneeling down. Sometimes we used to go out on school trips or just at weekends with a few friends, but whenever we were outside the school we had to wear a hat. There was one teacher who always used to give me extra homework because my socks weren't pulled up, and that was in the school late in the evening! I suppose it wasn't that bad, but at the time it felt like a prison! I kept getting into trouble for something. Most of the time I forgot something – normally my school badge. We had to wear that all the time, in the school and out, because it had our house colours on it.
Pat	Wow, that doesn't sound like much fun!
Gail	No, but it was a good education. I suppose....(fade out)

Listening **7.4** EXERCISE **3**

Fred	Hi, Cheryl.
Cheryl	Oh, hi. I tried phoning you earlier but there was no answer. Is your phone switched on?
Fred	What, my mobile? Yes. What time did you try ringing?
Cheryl	It must have been about an hour ago. I was going to ask you…
Wilma	Hello, you two.

Fred	Hi, Wilma.
Wilma	What were you going to ask, Fred?
Cheryl	Oh, nothing important, it's just that I couldn't get through to his mobile phone.
Wilma	Oh, mobile phones are a waste of time. Even if you do get through, it's always difficult to hear. And it sometimes starts ringing just when you don't want it to. Just see how many people drive their cars using them!
Cheryl	Well, yes, I suppose there are times when some people think they are annoying, but they're so useful. I couldn't live without mine.
Fred	No, same here. I use it for text messages more than anything though.
Wilma	The thing I really don't like about them is that people can reach you wherever you are, and sometimes you just want to get away. I mean, look at all these businessmen who use mobile phones and the Internet – it's like being at work 24 hours a day. There doesn't seem to be any privacy left. But then, I suppose that's becoming more common these days anyway.
Cheryl	What's becoming more common?
Wilma	People, you know, not respecting the privacy of others.
Cheryl	Oh, that's a bit strong, don't you think? I mean, it's just a mobile phone. And anyway, I think people respect privacy more than they used to.
Wilma	Well, look at the media then. If you're famous, then everything you do is photographed, written down or gossiped about.
Cheryl	Only celebrities. It's not like the press are always knocking on my door anyway.
Fred	Maybe not, but the reporters definitely don't respect people's privacy. They feel they have a right to know everything, no matter how personal. I don't think that's right, do you?
Cheryl	I suppose not, but in a democratic country…
Fred	Oh, don't start talking politics!
Cheryl	No, I was just going to say that people have a right to know what's happening.
Fred	What, even if it doesn't concern them?
Cheryl	Who decides whether it concerns the public or not? It should be our right to have access to all information and decide for ourselves.
Wilma	Well, interesting though this is, I have to go.
Cheryl	Yeah, me too. I'll see you later.
Wilma	Bye
Fred	Bye.

Listening 7.10 EXERCISE 3

Many younger people today do not regularly buy or even read a newspaper. A lot of what they know about the world is taken from television, the radio or the Internet. Although there is no great harm in this, it does signal a general decline in reading the written word. Computer games and other such pursuits have long since overtaken the idea of a book before bedtime. For the older generation, this can be hard to understand, yet it must be accepted that the world is entering into a considerably more technological age in which computer literacy is much more highly prized than having read any of the classic works of literature.

Listening 8.4   EXERCISE 1

It's **(1)** <u>not unusual</u> for passengers on an aeroplane, particularly first-time flyers, to feel trepidation prior to getting on the aircraft and nervousness during the flight, particularly on long-haul flights such as Australia to the UK. Yet the belief that flying is dangerous is a **(2)** <u>misconception</u>. Flying, **(3)** <u>not unlike</u> sky diving, is statistically much safer than many other daily activities like driving a car or even crossing the road.

Listening 8.4   EXERCISE 3

1   J: Hi Lyn. Do you like my new T-shirt?

    L: Mmm…it's very… bright, …isn't it?

2   No need to book, the man said. Huh. Typical.

3   M: Pat's travelling again. I think he travels too much, don't you, Steve?

    S: What, two holidays a year? Too much?

4   Well, if this is what they call luxury travel then I'd hate to see economy.

5   A 'high-quality product' the box says. Is that what you call 'high quality'?

6   I asked you to sit down, sir.

7   Well that steak was … interesting. Glad we bothered coming out for that.

Listening 8.4   EXERCISE 5

Travel agent	Hello. Welcome to the Travel Depot. How can I help you?
Client	Well, I'm looking for a reasonably priced holiday. I went to South Africa for a month last year and I'd like to see North America this time – maybe Canada, but I'm also interested in Europe if the prices to Canada are too expensive. I'm on quite a tight budget you see.
Travel agent	[doesn't sound convinced] Well, you could go to Europe but … I'll get some prices for Canada first. I've been to Vancouver, it's lovely at this time of year. And we have some special offers on at the moment.
Client	Okay, well, I have some relatives over in Vancouver so that would be good. I can always travel around Europe next year. Besides, it may be a bit too hot for me at this time.
Travel agent	Right, let's have a look at some prices then. When would you like to go?
Client	Some time at the end of next month if possible, but I'm quite flexible any time between the 24th and the 31st. I'd like to go for three weeks.
Travel agent	Well there's lots of availability for those dates. Now, if you're concerned about the cost, it's cheaper if you don't mind not flying direct.
Client	Sorry? What do you mean?
Travel agent	Well, if you don't mind changing planes then it's cheaper.
Client	Oh, well, I don't mind changing planes.
Travel agent	In that case, the cheapest flight I have leaves on the 25th and changes in New York. It's only a short stop – you'll be in the airport for two-and-a-half hours. How does that sound?
Client	Sounds good, but what's the price?
Travel agent	That's £412 for a return flight, but that doesn't include airport tax. Would you like to arrange any accommodation?

Client	No, I have a cousin I can stay with. All I need is the flight, so I think I'll take that one.
Travel agent	Right, I'll just check availability for your return. Three weeks did you say?
Client	Yes, that's right.
Travel agent	Okay … well there are seats available on the 14th or the 15th. Which one would you prefer?
Client	The 14th sounds good. Yes, from the 25th to the 14th sounds fine.
Travel agent	I'll reserve that for you then. Can you tell me your name please?
Client	Jim Jackson.
Travel agent	Is that J-A-C-K-S-O-N?
Client	That's right.
Travel agent	And can I take an address and contact number?
Client	Yes, it's 10 Allen Road, Oldham. Do you want a home number or my mobile?
Travel agent	Either's fine.
Client	Well, my home number is 0151 433 398.
Travel agent	OK, so you're booked on flight number VN217 to Vancouver, leaving London Heathrow at 11.35 in the morning on the 25th and returning on the 14th, so that's … 20 nights. Now, one more thing. Do you have any travel insurance? We recommend all our clients take out some kind of cover, even though most people don't end up needing it. Most people have it just for peace of mind.
Client	Well, what type of cover do you have?
Travel agent	There are two choices – the Gold Star and the Silver Star. Our most comprehensive cover is the Gold Star, which will cost £21 for the period you are away. It's a good policy because it covers almost all eventualities, even extreme sports such as snowboarding and skydiving.
Client	Hmm … What about the Silver Star?
Travel agent	That's £18, but it doesn't cover you for any dangerous sports.
Client	Well, for £3, I think I'll take the first one, the Gold cover please.
Travel agent	Right. And is there anything else I can help you with?
Client	Well, do you have any information about what to do in Vancouver?
Travel agent	Yes, I'm sure there's something on the computer that can help. Ahh, yes. There's a Shakespeare play at the theatre, but at $54 it's quite expensive. That starts at 8 p.m. The City Museum is really popular too, if you like that kind of thing. They have a special exhibition of Japanese armour next month. Entrance is free and the museum is open from 9.00 to 4.30 Monday to Saturday. Would you be interested in either of those?
Client	(sounds hesitant) Oh, well … errr, maybe.
Travel agent	Well, I'm sure you can arrange that when you get there anyway. So, it's the flight and the Gold Star insurance. That's … £433 in total.
Client	Can I pay by Visa?
Travel agent	Yes of course. If you start … (fade out)

Listening 8.10   EXERCISE 4

OK, when you arrive, you should come straight to the reception area. That's on your right as you enter the building. You need to bring some identification if you are going to take your driving test. After you have registered, you need to complete a theory test, so go out of the reception, walk straight down the corridor and turn right. On the left you will find the two theory test rooms. You should go into Room A – that's the first one up the corridor.

When you have finished your theory test, go to the processing room just opposite and give them your test papers. They will be graded by the time you have finished the practical test. You can go to the waiting area until you are called. That's behind the processing office, but you will have to go up the corridor and turn right, then right again. Follow the corridor to the end and the waiting area is on your left. It's a little confusing! Finally, you have the practice test area. Coming from the waiting room, you have to turn right three times and it's just in front of you. It's at the other end of the corridor from Theory test room B.

Oh, and if you need the toilet at any time, it's back down this way, beside the entrance. The door is facing the side of the processing office. Good luck!

Listening **8.10** EXERCISE 6

Joanna	Hello, sorry to bother you but my name's Joanna Griffith. Are you Gillian Davidson?
Gillian	Yes, I am. Did you say your name was Joanna? Nice to meet you. I understand I'm going to be your mentor here. Welcome to the university. Is it your first day here?
Joanna	Yes, well, kind of. I came in for an interview a while back and again yesterday for registration and orientation. I know the university offers a mentor system for new students, but I'm not too sure what that's about exactly.
Gillian	Well, I'm in my second year here and a number of students in our year have been elected to help new students settle in. You can ask us about anything you are not sure of, and of course it's a good way of making sure that new students get the chance to meet other people right from the start. It can sometimes be a little daunting trying to make friends when you don't know anyone, especially when you're starting a new course.
Joanna	Yes, that's true. I've only just moved down from Staffordshire, and everything is very new for me, so any help I can get is very much appreciated.
Gillian	Well, I hope you'll have a good time here. The teachers aren't *too* bad but the social life is great! I love it! So, do you have any questions I can answer for you?
Joanna	Well, first of all I need a little help with directions. It's so easy to get lost – it's not a small place, is it?
Gillian	Not at all, but you'll get used to it after a week or two. So where are you looking for in particular?
Joanna	Well, I'm majoring in business studies and I had a tour of the business school at orientation yesterday so that's not a problem, but one of my courses this year is sociology, so I need to know where the social science department is. Do you know where it is?
Gillian	Yes, sure. It's quite easy, actually. From here, just walk straight ahead to the end of the pathway – it's all pedestrianised in this part of the campus – then turn right at the end. It's the first building on the left. You can see it from here.
Joanna	Oh yes, that's great – thanks.
Gillian	No problem. Anything else?
Joanna	Well, I'll probably have lots of questions, but I can't think of anything right now.
Gillian	Well, if you do have anything you want to ask, then just come and find me. I'm in the library between 3 and 4 p.m. most days, except Mondays. I play volleyball then.
Joanna	Great.
Gillian	And don't forget that there is a party tonight for new students. It'll be a good opportunity for you to meet some other students from your year. I'll meet you here at 7.30 if you like and we can go together. It doesn't start until 8, so that'll give us plenty of time.
Joanna	OK, that sounds fine. Well, thanks for everything, and I'll see you later.

Listening 9.4 EXERCISE 4

Interviewer	Good afternoon. I have with me in the studio today Dr Stephen Philipps, author of the new book *Silver Lining*, which is an investigation into UFOs. Now, Dr Philipps, can you tell us a little about your book?
Dr Philipps	Yes, certainly. Over the last 12 years I have become increasingly interested in the subject of UFOs, and this book is a compilation of all the sightings I have heard about together with evidence. You see, so many people are convinced that there is life on other planets that I thought I would do some research myself.
Interviewer	And what did you find? Are we alone in the universe? (sceptical laugh)
Dr Philipps	You sound sceptical. Well, you'll have to buy the book to find out my personal conclusion, but I can tell you this – there are a lot of sightings in a number of different countries, and the surprising fact that I have found is that despite never having met each other, a great number of these 'witnesses' describe an almost identical object. Now I realise that television and the media has given us all a mental picture of a UFO. A silver ship with bright lights that moves at very high speed. What interested me was that in all the eye-witness accounts I heard, people gave very precise and detailed descriptions that varied only slightly. Reports from America, Europe – even Asia – all share a significant number of similarities.
Interviewer	Hmm. Interesting. Tell me, have you been able to see any evidence yourself?
Dr Philipps	Well, no. My aim in writing this book was not really to present my own opinion, but to gather all the information available and collate it into a kind of reference guide. Personally I don't have anything much to add apart from the conclusions that I've drawn from the accounts I've heard.
Interviewer	I understand that there is a strong body of opinion that claims there is hard evidence that is being suppressed by the American government. Could you comment on that?
Dr Philipps	Hmm. The second chapter of my book actually talks about a place in America that has often been in the media – Area 51.
Interviewer	Area 51?
Dr Philipps	Yes, it's a military base in New Mexico. In 1947, a man called MacBrazel claimed …
Interviewer	Sorry, who?
Dr Philipps	MacBrazel. That's M-A-C capital B-R-A-Z-E-L. Anyway, MacBrazel claimed to have found pieces of an alien spacecraft on his farm in Roswell. Now many people believe that this was true, and that the government of the time took the debris. Since that time they have denied all knowledge of any such find, and accounts by the many leading experts at the time dismissed the claim, believing that MacBrazel had actually found pieces of a high-altitude weather balloon that had disintegrated. Now the lack of information combined with the large number of conspiracy theorists means that no useful scientific conclusion can be drawn, but I have found out one or two surprising details. Again, you'll have to buy the book if you want to find out more.
Interviewer	OK. Now, I understand that an overwhelming majority of UFO sightings occurred in America. Do you find that in any way relevant?
Dr Philipps	Well, as I mentioned before, there are a large number of conspiracy theorists, and the popularity of science fiction programmes in America could lead you to suspect that these sightings may be nothing more than an overactive imagination. However, I have found that there are a number of other factors that determine UFO sightings. In northern Europe, the number of reports is very low, whereas in Southern Europe, where there is more open space, less light pollution and generally clearer skies, the number of sightings increases. Now when you consider the vast open areas of America, particularly around New Mexico, there is an argument that UFOs are simply easier to see in certain geographical and climatic situations.

Interviewer	Hmm. Well, I've never thought of that. If I could ask you one final question Dr Philipps … what about alien abduction?
Dr Philipps	Ahh. Well, I don't really cover that in my book. You see, I was looking to present facts from which people could draw their own conclusions. With these reported abductions, I found them to be very unreliable.
Interviewer	Well, thank you very much for your time. Before we finish, I'd just like to add that *Silver Lining* is available at all leading book stores, priced at nineteen pounds ninety nine. Until next week, goodbye.

Listening 9.4   EXERCISES   5–6

OK, I'd like to keep this meeting as brief as possible as I'm sure we all have things to do. I've asked you here just to remind you about this Friday's field trip. This is the first of many field trips you will be going on, so there are a few rules I'd like to make clear now. Most importantly, I want you all to remember that simply because you are leaving the college does not mean that you are not studying. This is an essential part of your course and should be treated as such. There will be two assignments for you to complete whilst you are there and some extension work you will be expected to do over the weekend, so I suggest you all pay attention on the day. Moving on, remember that we are going to a salt marsh and must dress appropriately. High-heeled shoes and T-shirts are not what I consider appropriate. You need good footwear, preferably boots, and you should bring a waterproof jacket as the weather is unpredictable. It would also be a good idea to bring a change of clothes. There is a chance you will get wet, and a three-hour return journey in damp clothes is nobody's idea of fun.

We will be on the marsh from about ten o'clock to about four, so you will be given a light lunch. However, if you want to bring any snacks with you, then please feel free to do so, although we will be stopping for dinner on the way home.

Now, this is the fourth time the college has been to Park Drive salt marsh, and so far we have never lost a student (*laughs*). However, remember that there are 28 people going, and if you are late you will be keeping myself and your colleagues waiting, and at that time of the morning you will not find me very forgiving. Please try to arrive a few minutes before seven. If you're not here on the hour you risk being left behind.

For those of you who are being collected in the evening, you can expect to be back here between 8.30 and 9 p.m., but do warn whoever may be coming for you that the traffic is unpredictable and it may well be later.

Before you go, I'll hand out your assignment papers and briefly explain what you have to do. (*Pause*) Now, on the first page, all you are required to do is identify the flora and fauna on the page and find an example in the salt marsh. As I told you on Monday, you will need a camera for this. I recommend one of those disposable cameras rather than something more valuable as the marsh can get very dirty. Now on page 2, you will be looking more at the birdlife on the marsh. You should be able to see what you have to do for this assignment, but there will be plenty of time on the way there to ask any other questions.

Well, we'll stop there and I'll see you all on Friday morning. Oh, before you go, just a word of caution – the plants are there to be seen and photographed only. Remember that this is a protected site and we have to get permission for this trip. If there are any problems, we may not be allowed to go again and you will be spoiling the opportunity for other students.

OK. If you have any questions, come and see me later today or tomorrow.

Listening **9.7** Test

Section 1

Receptionist	Good morning, Sir. How can I help you?
William	Hello. Is this Southern Rental Car?
Receptionist	Yes, it is.
William	I wonder if you could help me. I'm ringing from Nelson, but I'm coming over to Auckland for 12 days and I'd like to hire a car.
Receptionist	Okay, I'll fill in a booking for you now. First, can I take your name?
William	Yes, it's William Waddell.
Receptionist	Sorry, could you spell your surname?
William	Yes it's W-A-D-D-E-L-L.
Receptionist	Thanks. Now, can I have an address and phone number?
William	Sure. I live at 10 Robyn Place. That's R-O-B-Y-N Place.
Receptionist	And that's Nelson, isn't it?
William	That's right. Do you want my home number or my mobile?
Receptionist	Home number will be fine.
William	OK, it's (07) 263 8666.
Receptionist	Great. Now, can I also have a credit card number?
William	Do I have to pay by credit card?
Receptionist	Well, we need a credit card number as a guarantee. It's a standard policy for car rentals.
William	OK. Well, I'll pay by Visa then. The card number is 4550 … 1392 … 8309 … 3221.
Receptionist	And the expiry date?
William	Sorry?
Receptionist	Your card – when does it expire?
William	Oh, next July.
Receptionist	Right. Now, how long did you want the car for? Twelve days did you say?
William	No, I only need a car for 10 days, from the 2nd to the 11th of next month.

Receptionist	Now, what type of car are you looking to hire?
William	Well, I'm not too worried about the model of the car but I understand that you have rental cars from just $25 a day. Is that correct?
Receptionist	We do sometimes have the $25 deals, but only in the low season. For the period you are looking at, the cheapest we have is $35. However, that price includes unlimited kilometres.
William	Sorry, did you say unlimited kilometres? What does that mean exactly?
Receptionist	That means that no matter how far you go, the cost is the same. Some companies charge for rental and then charge again for every kilometre you actually drive.
William	Well I am going to be travelling quite long distances – I'm visiting relatives and they live quite far apart from each other, so unlimited kilometres are probably a good idea.
Receptionist	If you're travelling long distances, you would be better off with an automatic. Changing gears in a manual can make it more expensive on petrol.
William	OK, I'll take the automatic then.

Receptionist	Right. So that's an automatic car for 10 days from the 2nd to the 11th. That's all booked. Is there anything else I can help you with?
William	No that's fine. Oh, sorry – what do I need to bring with me when I pick up the car?
Receptionist	All you need is your driving licence.
William	Right, well thanks very much. Bye.

Listening **9.7** Test

Section 2

When thinking about beautiful countryside or stunning views, it has long been accepted that Australia and New Zealand have few equals. What is perhaps slightly less well known is what these countries can offer to the avid train enthusiast. Both countries have railways which pass through breathtaking scenery in the utmost of comfort.

In New Zealand you can travel from the country's biggest city, Auckland, to where a third of the population lives, its capital, Wellington, on the longest passenger rail service in the country – the Overlander. Crossing 681 kilometres, the train winds through the lush farmland of the Waikato and up the Raurimu Spiral onto an amazing 'volcanic plateau' surrounded by native bush. On a clear day you will be able to see three of New Zealand's most famous volcanoes – Mount Ruapehu, Mount Ngauruhoe and Mount Tongariro. The whole journey can be completed in 11 hours, but for those keen to see a little more of the country, the trip can be extended over three or four days. This gives travellers the opportunity of seeing the famous Waitomo caves, relaxing in the mud pools of Rotorua, or skydiving over Lake Taupo.

Moving on to the South Island, you can take the Transalpine through the Southern Alps, travelling from the South Pacific Ocean to the Tasman Sea. Climbing from Christchurch right into the alps, this 223 km trip is particularly impressive as the train passes through 16 tunnels before descending to Greymouth at the end of the line. Taking only five hours, this is a relatively short trip, but it is worth noting that this journey has been listed as the sixth most scenic rail route in the world. For those that are not so keen on mountains, the South Island has a second option – the Transcoastal. With the sea on one side and the mountains on the other, it again shows some of the best scenery New Zealand has to offer. Also taking five hours, one of the highlights of this journey is the opportunities for whale watching. The fortunate few that see whales are well rewarded, but there are more common sights which are just as enjoyable, such as penguins and seals.

Although these three train journeys are undeniably breathtaking, some travellers prefer the longer journeys on offer in Australia. The Indian Pacific, for example, which travels from Sydney through to Perth and has been dubbed 'the adventure that spans Australia'. With three nights on board, the train takes in the Blue Mountains and the Nullarbor Plains, and, as the name implies, the Indian Pacific shows you two oceans. This train journey holds two world records: covering 4352 km, it is one of the world's longest train journeys. It also travels the world's longest straight stretch of railway track (478 km). For those who find these distances a little daunting, passengers can stretch their legs at a number of different stops such as Kalgoorlie, famous for gold, and Broken Hill, first founded as a silver mine.

If three days on board a train seems a little excessive, there are alternatives. The Ghan for example, which travels from Adelaide in the south to Alice Springs in the centre of the continent, taking 20 hours. Passing through Crystal Brook, Port Augusta and Woomera, this journey gives an indication of what life was like for the earlier settlers as they discovered the country. Along the way, you can also see the Iron Man sculpture, which was constructed by railway workers to commemorate the one millionth concrete sleeper laid during construction of the line.

Finally, just a quick word about the Overland, which runs between Melbourne and Adelaide. As the first train to travel between the capitals of two states, it is a historic as well as relaxing way to travel, and is famous for being the oldest long-distance train journey on the continent.

With so many memorable journeys to choose from, the only problem you will have is knowing which one to do first.

Listening **9.7** Test

Section 3

Miley	Hi Lyn. How's your project coming along?
Lyn	Oh, not very well. I've got all the information, but I can't seem to organise it into a presentation.
Miley	Well you'd better hurry. You only have one more week.
Lyn	Yes, that's OK, it's just that … ohh … (sound of desperation).
Miley	Well, why don't you try your presentation on me. Maybe I can help.
Lyn	Really? Great! OK, well, I've chosen solar power for my subject, and I'm going to talk specifically about domestic water heating. You know, like the ones popular in America. I've got some facts here.
Miley	That's good, but just start your presentation from the beginning.
Lyn	Oh, right. Here we go then. There are many reasons why we should be looking elsewhere for energy sources. As most people are aware, fossil fuels and other such non-renewable sources are by definition finite, so something needs to be in operation soon. Currently, there are a number of alternative energy sources available which can, with a little preparation, be used to provide for a significant part of our domestic energy requirements. In this presentation I am focusing on solar power and its application as a domestic water heater. As a renewable energy source, solar power is in many ways ideal. The amount of the sun's energy which reaches the Earth every minute exceeds the energy that the global population consumes in a year. Although scientists argue that it is not finite, sunlight is certainly a long-lasting resource which is not depleted through use, and solar power converters use this energy without needing any complex moving parts. Once collected and stored, solar energy can be used for many purposes, but it is becoming increasingly popular as a domestic heating source. Generally a building that is heated by solar power will have its water heated by solar power as well, and this has even worked in areas that are not exposed to long hours of direct sunlight such as the United Kingdom, although not so well as in warmer climates … (long pause)
Miley	Why have you stopped?
Lyn	Well, that's all I've got so far.
Miley	Oh. Well, start by talking about how effective it is.
Lyn	Oh, OK. Well, there are a number of factors that influence how efficient solar power can be. The first, obviously, is the amount of sunlight, and this is dependent on season, time of day, and climate. Although the UK has something of a bad reputation for sunshine, it is actually quite productive during some parts of the year. Given a sufficient size of solar panel and water storage tank, solar power can provide all of our water-heating requirements in June and July, and even provide the majority until October. From October to the end of the year, this figure falls dramatically. December is the least productive, being able to supply less than 5% of the average household's hot water requirement. It is at this point that solar power needs to be supplemented with a more traditional form of heating. From January

solar power becomes more effective at a rate of about 20% per month, although this rise decelerates to around 18% by May.

Miley	Now say something about this water heater. Do you have any information about that?
Lyn	Yes, I've got an illustration of a water tank here.
Miley	That's good, but you'll have to describe it.
Lyn	Right. Well, the ideal water tank in the UK has a capacity of 45 to 50 litres, but must be at least 40 litres to be effective. The solar coil is put in the bottom of the tank to heat the water. Now, remember that solar-heated water will not get quite as hot as fossil fuel water heaters. The bottom half of the tank is normally 20 degrees, and this is why it is important not to have a tank that is too large as it would take too much energy to heat. In this illustration, it rises to 40 degrees from halfway up. Don't forget that hot water rises, so the top third of the tank is the hottest, and reaches an average temperature of 65 degrees.
Miley	And what's this second layer around the tank?
Lyn	Oh that's insulation. Because the tank is often either outside or just under the roof, rigid foam is used as an insulation layer. It should be at least 80 mm thick all around.
Miley	That seems like a good presentation. All you need to do is to prepare some short notes and a larger illustration so you can use it as a demonstration and you'll be fine.
Lyn	You think so? Well, thanks very much for the help. Maybe I can do the same for you one day.
Miley	Maybe. Anyway, I have to go. Good luck!
Lyn	Thanks. Bye.

Listening **9.7** Test

Section 4

Interviewer	Continuing our theme of business marketing, I have with me today Mr Brian Kinsella, who is here to talk about the differences between marketing a product and marketing a service.
Brian Kinsella	Good morning. Now I understand that many of you here today are interested in a career in services marketing. Well I have been the marketing director for Oceania Travel for nearly 11 years, so I feel that I can present what I consider to be the most important aspects of marketing a service. However, before I begin, I want to clarify what I mean by services marketing. This not only means aspects like holiday destinations but also professional services such as legal advice. In short, anyone that sells a service.

Actually, a lot of the traditional services such as lawyers, accountants, etc. have not felt too comfortable marketing their services. It's almost perceived in industries such as these that the need to market indicates a weakness in the services provided. However, more and more such industries are realising the importance of marketing to sustain their customer numbers, especially when their competitors are marketing themselves.

Now, the main difference between marketing a product and a service is that the customers cannot understand exactly what the service will be. They can see a product and can comprehend exactly what that product will do for them. A service is more intangible – by that I mean whatever each customer gains from the service is often very personal. For example, with a travel agency, clients choose to travel abroad for a multitude of motives. Some people travel overseas for the experience and really want to get to know the culture of the local people. Others wish to escape from reality, totally relax in sophisticated comfort and be waited on hand and foot. |

Obviously, our clients will not be judging what we offer by the same standards, and travel agents, like other such service industries, have an extremely difficult job in satisfying a range of customers from diverse backgrounds with different expectations.

Our company has overcome this dilemma in a number of ways. First of all, our travel consultants are given extensive training in customer service and buyer behaviour. Our aim is not just to be a profit-making organisation, but also to meet and exceed the expectations or dreams of our clients. Our mission statement, in fact, is primarily to offer a service which is above and beyond the hopes of our clients. In addition, we regularly visit the tourist destinations we promote and inform all of our staff about any changes in specific areas.

Not only is it important to be fully informed about every possible aspect of the service you are marketing, it is also essential to constantly improve the service offered. At Oceania Travel, we regularly conduct surveys with all of the people that visit our resorts of choice. Any negative feedback we try to remedy at once. Our clients are met by a company representative during their stay, and we have a set procedure for dealing with any complaints. Our clients are not expected to have to approach the hotel reception, as we have a 24-hour contact service direct to our representatives, and this representative should always welcome any customer problems or questions. In the event of a complaint, the representative will then try to remedy the complaint with the hotel. If the problem cannot be rectified by the hotel manager, our representative is authorised to remedy the situation him or herself. For situations beyond the representative's authority, our complaints department is contacted. The complaints department guarantees a solution within the day. If the customer is still not satisfied, they are welcome to approach our head office on their return.

So you see that marketing a service is catering more for the clients' expectations than anything else and it is that which makes services marketing a very intricate business. Now that's the end of my presentation, but if there is anything you want to ask, then please feel free to do so. Thank you.

Listening 9.10 EXERCISE 3

Teacher	So Eileen, tell me how you felt just before your test.
Student	Well, it was the first time I had taken a test for such a long time that I was very nervous. Actually, I didn't sleep very well for nearly a week before the test. I felt a little under pressure because a friend of mine had just got his results a week before, and he'd done very well. Anyway, I rang my parents the night before, and my mother reminded me that there was no point in worrying, and that made me feel a little calmer.
Teacher	So tell me how things went on the day. What about the listening test?
Student	Surprisingly, the listening test wasn't as difficult as I'd thought. The hardest part was spelling, but I didn't feel that the sections got much more difficult as the test went on. By the end I felt quite confident in my answers.
Teacher	Tell me about the speaking. What was that like?
Student	I didn't make a very good start. From the waiting area, I was supposed to go up to the end of the corridor and turn right. My interview room was on the right, but I went in the room on the left and when I showed the interviewer my ID he told me I was in the wrong room! Anyway, he took me where I was supposed to go so it wasn't too bad. Anyway, my real interviewer was great! She made me feel so relaxed. Before the interview began, she asked me if I'd taken the test before, and when I told her this was my first

time, she just smiled and said 'relax'. I did find myself getting a little nervous, but I just took a breath and relaxed. As for the actual interview, I felt that I could have done a little better, but then I suppose most people feel that. Once or twice I realised I'd made a mistake so I just corrected myself and went on.

Teacher	Okay. What about the writing test?
Student	Well, I spent a few minutes too long on Task One – I had to write about a table, and I was hoping for a graph because they're easier to write about. Actually, I think tables are the most difficult. Task Two wasn't too bad though because the title was similar to something I had studied in my class. I wrote a plan, so I just followed what I had written. Near the end I changed a few parts of the plan and didn't follow my original idea but I still felt that I'd done a good job.
Teacher	And finally, then, the reading?
Student	Well, when the examiner handed out the test, I thought the size of the booklet was a little intimidating. To calm me down, I had a quick look through the three passages before I began, and didn't have much problem with the first and the third, but I thought Reading Passage 2 was quite difficult. There were some multiple-choice questions, and I've always found them a little difficult. But I just left them and moved on, and found I had a few minutes at the end to go back and answer them.
Teacher	Good. Well, just before we finish, do you have any advice you would give to someone just about to take their test?
Student	Yes, a couple of things actually. A few days before the test, look through the work you have done, but the night before the test, don't do anything. Relax and go to bed early. In the morning, have a good breakfast. But the most important advice I would give is to avoid speaking or listening to anything but English on the day. Listen to the radio when you get up, and take a portable cassette player to listen to when you're waiting to go into the test room. Don't speak your native language even if there are people that you know at the test centre.
Teacher	Well, thanks very much, Eileen. When do you get your results?
Student	Next Friday, I think.
Teacher	I hope you've done well.
Student	Thanks.

Model essays

Unit 1.2 `EXERCISE 10` (page 8)

Visa regulation should be relaxed for overseas students. Do you agree or disagree?

For many people interested in studying abroad, one of the first problems they face is obtaining a visa to enter the country and, in many situations, the procedure is time-consuming and frustrating. As a result, there is a clear case for making visa applications less stringent. However, there is also a potential for abuse if the system was made more lenient, and both of these opinions need to be considered.

In support of simplifying the visa-application procedure, it must be remembered that obtaining a visa is one of the first steps towards studying in a foreign country. If this process is difficult then it reflects poorly on the country the student is intending to go to. Moreover, once in the country, students often find it less problematic to use the services of an immigration agent, to whom they surrender their passports and pay sometimes phenomenal sums of money. In the same way, this again reflects poorly on the host country.

Yet there is a point of view that suggests visa regulations should remain as they are, or even become stricter. It is inevitable that once a developed country opens its door to students, there will be some who exploit the opportunity without any intention of fulfilling the study requirements of their visa.

To conclude, perhaps the best solution would be to allow the schools, colleges and universities that attract international students to have greater control over those students that do arrive in a country. This would allow the institutions themselves to police the students while being overseen by the Immigration Service itself.

(262 words)

Unit 1.8 `EXERCISE 6` (page 21)

The graph shows trends in a European city in four different types of accommodation position over a thirty-year period.

The most striking trend is the overall decline in the number of people having bought, or in the process of buying, their own property, falling by approximately 20 000 from 1970 to 1980, and then to approximately 15 000 by 1990. There was a slight recovery by 2000. There is an inverse relationship between this number and those represented by the category 'other', becoming more apparent after 1980.

A similar correlation can be observed between the number of tenants and the number of landlords, with nearly 50 000 tenants and just over 10 000 fewer landlords in 1980. From that point to 2000, both numbers declined, although the number of landlords declined at a marginally faster rate.

Overall, all categories of accommodation declined over the period, with the sharpest decline coming from those buying a property.

(155 words)

Unit 1.11 EXERCISE 7 (page 26)

Individuals should not be allowed to carry guns.

There are some who hold the opinion that gun ownership should be restricted, as it is in many countries, and that people in general should not be permitted to keep them. This is an opinion I personally strongly support for the following reasons.

A major reason why governments should not allow people to have guns is because of the potential for accidents. In America, for example, you can legally shoot people if you find them robbing your house, but this can lead to people dying over cases of mistaken identity. In addition, there are crimes where people act rashly or in anger, so guns that were intended for defence are often used aggressively.

There is also the intentional damage caused by guns. It is statistically evident that the number of gun-related crimes is higher in countries where firearm ownership is legal. Countries like America, for example, suffer from a disproportionately high number of fatal shootings in comparison with most other countries.

Some people, however, argue that shooting is a sport, thus being prevented from owning their own firearm is both unjust and a violation of our rights. Yet this must be balanced with the overwhelming number of people who use guns for criminal purposes.

To sum up, it is clear that the proliferation of guns leads to injury and death both intentionally and unintentionally. Although there are points to support gun ownership, they are weak in comparison with the rising tide of gun crime, a situation which will only continue to worsen.

(252 words)

Unit 2.2 EXERCISE 5 (page 33)

The bar chart illustrates three factors of popular sports in a typical city in Europe, namely sport type, number of spectators in attendance and different age categories.

The most notable trend is that people aged between 15 and 25 always ranked the lowest regardless of sport. The graph shows that in this age category, golf was not watched at all, and athletics and cricket were not popular. Soccer attracted the most spectators for this age range, closely followed by rugby.

Those people aged 41 or over accounted for the highest number of spectators of most sports, particularly in golf and cricket. Rugby and athletics, however, were favoured by those in the middle category, aged between 26 and 40, being the clear majority of rugby spectators.

Of all the sports, cricket and golf showed the widest disparity between the age groups, with soccer being the sport that drew an almost even number of spectators.

(153 words)

Unit 2.5 EXERCISE 1 (page 37)

Advances in technology and automation have reduced the need for manual labour. Therefore working hours should be reduced. To what extent do you agree?

In many production-oriented factories, machinery has evolved to such a degree that the demand for physical labour has considerably reduced, leading to the suggestion of a reduced working week. However, there are several factors that need to be considered.

Primarily, the long-term impact of shorter working weeks needs to be considered. Although less time at work may sound appealing, the reality is that people may find that they have too much free time. Fewer working hours would presumably mean less income, so a situation arises where employees have more leisure time than their income can support. This has the potential to result in feelings of boredom, frustration or anxiety, all of which have potential side-effects for society as a whole.

Connected with this comes the social factor of self-esteem. Working less is one thing; working less because robots can complete the tasks you were assigned is another.

A solution that would benefit all those concerned would be to utilise the time no longer required for manual labour for something more productive. Instead of simply reducing the working week, a combination of industry and government support could allow for employees to receive further education and training, giving those employed in manual labour the academic tools to find different employment. Even automated factories still require technicians, mechanics and designers to maintain and improve production.

To summarise, until such time as automation has reduced the working week for all types of employee, it would perhaps be counter-productive to reduce the working week of those involved in manual labour without providing an alternative simply because they are replaceable.

(264 words)

Unit 2.8 EXERCISE 6 (page 44)

Comparing four different occupations in 1998, the chart illustrates the impact of illness due to stress and its correlation to days absent from work for both sexes.

The most obvious point is that men rated higher than women across the chart, with the most striking difference coming from those employed as fire fighters. In this occupation, men took more than three times as many days off, averaging 14 days in the year compared with four days for women. A similar trend can be observed with police officers, with men being absent for nearly twice the number of days.

The result for factory workers and teachers is not so pointed, but still with women taking fewer days off than men. For both groups, the difference between the sexes was only one day a year. Stress-related absence from work only accounted for one day a year for women in factory positions, rising to three for teachers. Men were absent for two days and four days respectively.

(164 words)

Unit 3.2 EXERCISE 7 (page 57)

The table gives opinions on recycling in percentages of people in six different age categories.

At less than 10 per cent, those under 15 and over 71 represent the lowest percentage of people that actively recycle. This figure increased over five-fold to 59 per cent for those aged 15 to 25. The remaining age categories varied between just under half to over one-third of people.

The under 15s represent the largest per cent of people who do not know about recycling. The lowest percentage was those aged 26 to 40, although this figure doubled to eight per cent for those just under this age. Slightly more than a quarter of those aged 56 to 70 knew nothing about recycling, a figure which is four times higher than those aged 41 to 55.

One-fifth of people aged 41 to 55 opted not to give their opinions on recycling, with those under 15 just one per cent behind. The remaining four categories were within a four per cent range.

(167 words)

Unit 3.5 EXERCISES 4-6

Modern appliances in the home have become more common, leaving no doubt that advances in technology have improved our lifestyle. Do you agree or disagree?

The impact of innovations and inventions in our daily lives has increased dramatically. Most homes these days have, at the very least, a washing machine and a microwave, yet this has had both positive and negative effects. Although there are definitely some improvements (it would now be difficult to live without them), the negatives are equally definable.

Primarily, the fact that these appliances have to be paid for, serviced, repaired and replaced means that we need to work to maintain this cycle. For example, in some countries the average washing machine is two or three weeks' wages for most people. Considering the product's life span, it can be estimated that we are working at least two or three days a year simply to cover the cost of the appliance, a calculation which is multiplied by all the appliances we acquire.

In addition, an increasing number of appliances are for purposes that were not previously considered necessities, but through marketing techniques, manipulative advertising and human nature we are now keen to acquire them. Electric juice makers are a perfect example.

Of course, there are appliances which in their basic format have improved our lifestyle simply because of the labour they save. The washing machine, which saves hours every week on handwashing, is an example of this. It is only when such appliances develop functions beyond their basic use, that they become more expensive but more desirable because of the addition of these extra functions that most of us never use.

It can therefore be concluded that only by carefully considering the use and relevance of the appliances we buy, can we say that they have improved our lifestyle.

(274 words)

Unit 3.8 EXERCISE 7 (page 68)

The table provides data about the use and production of natural gas in nine different countries in 2001.

The most striking trend can be seen in the USA, where figures are over five times higher than those of any other country. With the exception of the former Soviet Union, other countries' production figures were higher than their consumption figures, although there are no figures provided for either Japan or South Korea.

New Zealand had the lowest consumption and the closest correlation to its production, with 0.2 million tonnes excess. In contrast, the former Soviet Union accounted for far less production than it did consumption, using nearly 18 times the amount it produced. Australia produced nearly one-third more natural gas than it consumed. The United Kingdom produced over 10 million tonnes more than it used, twice the excess produced by the United Arab Emirates. China consumed only 0.7 million tonnes less than its production.

Although the majority of countries produced more gas than they used in the same year, the rate of both production and consumption was markedly different between them.

(180 words)

Unit 3.11 EXERCISE 9 (page 73)

> **It is the responsibility of governments to ensure that environmentally friendly policies are adopted. To what extent do you agree?**
>
> The general public has become increasingly aware of environmental issues, and this has led to a demand from some that the government become more involved. Indeed, it could be argued that green issues have been excessively debated. While I admit that concern for the environment is very important, a more relaxed approach to problems may have better results.
>
> One significant way in which environmentally sound policies could be followed is by a better standard of education about the issues in question. Granted, this approach may take a degree of organising, but educating not just children but whole communities would perhaps be more of an incentive than simply passing new laws.
>
> Naturally some people would argue that without passing laws which are enforceable, people would not actively become involved in more environmental approaches. This is true to a point, although I personally believe that people often act only in self-interest and therefore only by education will people fully understand that environmental protection is in their own long-term interest.
>
> Balancing this, there is a point beyond which even dedicated communities cannot lead to a better environment, such as in the field of industry. It is on this scale that the government should be legislating, making it financially viable for industry to operate as cleanly as possible.
>
> To summarise, the government should use its authority to govern industrial pollution but should at the same time encourage a better standard of education. By having an industrial and community plan, it would be considerably easier to embrace more environmentally sound policies.
>
> (256 words)

Unit 4.5 REVIEW (page 83)

> **The difference between popular culture and more traditional culture is vast. Discuss.**
>
> The modern and the traditional are often seen, if not as exact opposites, then at least as areas of contrast, and many people hold this to be true of culture. Although there are clear points to support this opinion, there are also a significant number of points of comparison, as I will now discuss.
>
> The culture of today revolves heavily around changes in technology. Mobile phones, for instance, have become an almost essential part of younger people's lives, and in this regard it can be said to be an example of the difference. Yet under the surface, we can see that this modern trend is actually little more than another method of communication, albeit less personal than speaking face-to-face.
>
> In a similar way, we can see home computers and the Internet, a clear part of modern culture, as simply an extension of reading. Simply because we now use a monitor and mouse rather than a book does not really make the two incomparable.
>
> There are some that claim technology is making us less sociable, that culturally we are isolating ourselves with modern appliances. Yet it must be understood that we are now in the age of the global village, a world wide web which allows us to interact with people from almost any country.
>
> In conclusion, it is not that the cultures of the past and today are so different, it is simply that the methods we use to express those cultures have changed. A culture should be flexible, adapting itself to each new generation; if not, then its worth is limited only to historians.
>
> (265 words)

Unit 4.11 EXERCISE 8 (page 94)

> **In many countries, government sponsorship of the arts costs millions in taxpayers' money. There are many more important things to spend money on. Do you agree?**
>
> There are some who claim that it is important to maintain the arts, and an equal number of people who are opposed to continued government funding. I will argue in favour of this latter point for a number of reasons.
>
> The strongest point is that money spent on the arts could have been used for considerably more vital purposes. While I admit that the arts are important to a country's identity, it must also be given that a nation's health and wellbeing should be paramount. The idea that elderly people are forced to wait for essential operations whilst the money required to increase available medical provision is spent on opera and ballet is plainly immoral.
>
> In addition to health concerns, there are also more deserving social causes for the money that should be considered before the arts. Homelessness, unemployment, single mothers, the crime rate – all of these issues deserve to be addressed before money is spent on what is essentially little more than entertainment.
>
> A third factor is that some people have no interest in preserving or funding the arts, feeling that they have little practical value. If the arts are so much in need of sponsorship, then perhaps this is a reflection of their lack of popularity, in which case they should not be supported. The money could go to more popular events instead.
>
> For each of these reasons, it can be concluded that there is little reason to continue funding the arts. Yet perhaps a compromise could be reached by which those keen to maintain the arts could raise a percentage of their own funds and the government could reduce its level of sponsorship.
>
> (276 words)

Unit 5.2 EXERCISE 4 (page 102)

> In both plans a proposed site for a hospital has been marked, and there are a number of similarities and differences between the proposed sites.
>
> Both are situated beside a main road and have a car park, although in plan A the car park is slightly further from the suggested site. In plan B, the main road terminates at the car park, whereas in the first plan it continues. Added to this, the route of the main road passes much closer to the hospital site which could cause problems due to traffic noise. On the other hand, plan A also has access by train, even though the station is half a kilometre away and requires crossing a main road.
>
> Around the site, both plans have natural features. In plan B there is a mountainous area and a river but these may be less accessible than the park and lake offered in plan A.
>
> Overall, plan A is superior because of the amenities it allows for patients, staff and visitors.
>
> (169 words)

Unit 6.5 EXERCISE 5 (page 132)

What factors do you think are important in promoting a higher standard of education?

Globally, there is an increasing requirement for ever-higher levels of education, with many students opting to study overseas to ensure they have the best available opportunities. This has been the result of a number of both external and internal influences as I will now present.

Internally, there have been a number of definable factors. With the governments of most nations eager to have more educated citizens, more funding has also been allocated to education. Given this, it follows that there is the potential for increased resources, which would then inevitably allow for a higher educational level. Better teacher training, thus allowing for better teachers, has also been influential.

Externally, the job market to have qualifications and certificates, often at the expense of experience, has resulted in pressure from students to raise the educational level. With many industries and companies becoming increasingly specialised, there has also been a demand for equally specialised courses and higher education programmes. This in turn has led to a higher standard of education. In addition, the majority of people find a correlation between their expected salary and their educational achievements, and this naturally acts as a factor in promoting further education.

One final factor which can be considered is that a higher standard of education has been directly affected by abusing the government's interest in educating its citizens, as this allows for people to remain studying for some considerable time with the only goal being to maintain a stress-free life for the student.

In conclusion, it can be observed that there are a number of both internal and external factors contributing to a higher level of education.

(271 words)

Unit 6.11 EXERCISE 6 (page 142)

A course of study that has no direct employment opportunities serves no purpose. To what extent do you agree with the above?

For many people, the main purpose of education is to provide the necessary knowledge and training to obtain a job, yet there are also people who hold that any further education can be said to have potential in the job market. Agreeing with this latter view, I will now support the opinion.

Primarily, there is the difficulty in knowing exactly which course of study would have clear employment possibilities. For those students opting to study arts subjects such as English literature, there is no direct path; potential opportunities could include becoming a librarian, author or teacher, but none of these can be said to be direct. Yet there is undeniable value in studying these subjects, as they allow for a more open-minded view of the world, an attitude which could later be useful in a business setting.

Another point to consider is the job market itself. With many industries in a constant state of evolution, studying for a particular path of employment may be redundant as the industry could well have changed direction by the time of graduation. Moreover, at the time of entering university, the majority of people do not have a clear career path laid out and thus they choose those study courses that appeal to them rather than those that offer a clear future.

To sum up, perhaps the best solution would be to adopt a more developed system of apprenticeship and work training, so that students can be moulded alongside changes in the industry, while those students with unfocused or general employment plans can continue with the current system.

(262 words)

Unit 7.2 EXERCISE 5 (page 148)

Journalists often claim that people have the right to know everything. Are there any situations in which the freedom of the press should be limited?

Freedom of information is considered to be an indication of an open and democratic country, yet this claim is often abused by those in the media as a way of exploiting people or situations. There are many cases in which journalistic freedoms are taken too far and some clear cases in which this should be limited.

Primarily, national security must be considered. If an elected government is appointed the task of governing the country, there are likely to be times when information must be considered secret for the good of the nation. There has been a recent case, for example, where British troop movements in a hostile country were published in a British newspaper.

In addition, there is also the personal aspect to consider. Journalists, especially for the tabloid papers, are not concerned about the mental and emotional anguish they might cause with certain stories. For example, people who have suffered a personal tragedy or loss are followed, questioned and photographed at a time when they are emotionally vulnerable. It is for the protection of such individuals or families that freedom of the press should face limitations.

However, there are occasions when misdemeanours or crimes have only come to light through investigative journalism. It is unlikely that any government would publicly acknowledge an error if it was felt it would otherwise not become common knowledge.

Overall, it would seem that limitations put on freedom of the press should be based on respect for the consequences, a situation that would be best served by limiting media access only to what will not cause undue harm.

(264 words)

Unit 7.5 EXERCISE 5 (page 151)

As we move into the digital age, books and newspapers are becoming less important. Within the next 20 years, computers will have entirely replaced any other such form of media. To what extent do you agree with the above?

There is little doubt that computers and the Internet have had an effect on more traditional forms of media, but it is unlikely that these more contemporary forms will be the only option available within 20 years.

Consider, for example, the impact television had in the mid-1900s, and the fears that this would lead to the end of more traditional pastimes like reading. Yet books remain popular across all generations. For many employees, computers have become a part of their working day, and as such they are not so keen to use them at home as well. Packing for a holiday, sitting by the bed, in the garden on a warm summer's day – these are all situations where books have remained, and almost certainly will remain, the media of choice. Even amongst the young, there has been something of a resurgence of interest in reading, as the Harry Potter phenomenon illustrated.

The future for newspapers, however, is less clear. Certainly there is something of a ritual about collecting and reading the morning paper, be it over breakfast or on the way to work, but there is a clear possibility that the Internet, offering the most up-to-date news, the clearest pictures and the widest coverage, will soon replace this.

To summarise, therefore, while there have been rapid developments in the field of computing, I personally do not believe that the technology of today and the media of the past are mutually exclusive. As such it is unlikely that we will see the disappearance of traditional media, and certainly of books, within the next 20 years.

(264 words)

Unit 7.8 EXERCISE 5 (page 156)

The diagram illustrates the process of developing a manuscript into a published book. The process begins with the initial writing, which is then sent to a publishing house for assessment. If necessary, the material is then returned for revisions by the writer and this cycle of the process is repeated until it passes the assessment stage. Following that, the project is discussed in pre-production meetings. Once a schedule has been arranged, a team is brought together for production, and the work is edited and produced in galley stage. This goes to the editor and the writer, following which illustrations are commissioned and the work is checked by the author and editor. This is then converted into first page proofs which are once again checked by both the editor and author before moving on to second page proofs. The process is concluded when these proofs are sent to the printer.

(149 words)

Unit 7.11 EXERCISE 6 (page 163)

Children watch too much television. As a result they are losing important social skills. What can be done about this?

For many working parents, a quick and simple solution to keeping their child occupied involves simply sitting them in front of the television, and many people have pointed out the potential loss of other skills that excessive television viewing can cause. However, this argument is flawed in a number of respects, as I will now explain.

Learning how to behave within society is first acquired by copying the actions of those around us. Traditionally, this was generally from parents or siblings, but as single-parent families and one-child families have become more common, it is inevitable that other sources are needed, and for this the television has a constructive purpose. This is compounded by the fact that while society in general is becoming more multicultural, this is not necessarily true of families. Television offers children exposure to other races, nationalities and perspectives which they might otherwise not have had.

The argument that children become less creative through watching television is also inaccurate; children have been able to learn from what they watch, like how to make rockets from washing-up liquid bottles and binoculars from kitchen roll tubes. Added to this, programmes watched can give children a common topic of conversation.

In conclusion, there is a definite case to be built against the assumption that television has a negative influence on children's social abilities. Yet there is also some justification for concern in situations where parents allow children to view programmes which are unintended and unsuitable for them. What is needed is careful monitoring of what children watch.

(256 words)

Unit 8.5 ⬛EXERCISE 4⬛ (page 177)

> **Traffic congestion in major cities is an increasing problem, yet there is an environmental impact to be considered when building new roads. What can be done about this problem?**
>
> It is a well-known fact that of all the animal species on earth, humans are the most environmentally damaging. Traffic pollution is getting worse, yet simply creating more roads (while technically possible) has even more of a negative effect on the land, therefore other possibilities need to be considered.
>
> One of the more obvious solutions to the problem would be to improve public transport and raise the expense of driving our own cars. Either by control or by funding, local governments could ensure that public transport becomes the most economical method of commuting to work. In one European country, local governments have pursued this scheme and the results have been so successful that they have actually reduced the number of roads into the city.
>
> Another potential solution is to encourage working from home. The technology is readily available for most of us to do so, and is likely to be popular with a high percentage of employees. The introduction of more flexible working hours is also a possibility that, although not actually leading to fewer cars on the road, would help congestion problems.
>
> In many countries, local transport authorities have erected signs that provide information about road conditions, giving drivers the opportunity to find less congested routes to their destination. This system could be improved by more advanced technology in cars themselves.
>
> Regardless of the final solution, it is becoming increasingly clear that traffic pollution is not simply a local issue but a global one, and unless alternative strategies are put into effect soon the damage may be irreversible.
>
> (258 words)

Unit 8.8 ⬛EXERCISE 5⬛ (page 182)

> **The number of car accidents is increasing annually. This is the result of poor driving habits. To what extent do you agree?**
>
> When reading a local newspaper, it is common to see articles about serious car crashes. The reasons for car crashes vary, but at its root the problem is usually bad driving.
>
> It has also become more common over the last decade to travel longer and longer distances – journeys which can cause fatigue in drivers. Such accidents arising from this situation are the result of not adhering to the practice of taking breaks and therefore poor driving habits are to blame. The same indirect cause can be seen when bad weather is blamed for accidents and yet the driver did not allow for the conditions of the road in either the speed or manner of his or her driving.
>
> Developments in car production have also indirectly led to accidents. Despite cars becoming ever safer, they have also become faster, with better acceleration and, for impatient or inconsiderate drivers, this has led to problems. This can be witnessed at most intersections; stopping on an orange light is an increasingly rare thing for a driver.
>
> Yet there is a point that needs to be included when considering the cause of accidents: the number of vehicles on the road is rising, and therefore a rise in the number of car accidents is statistically inevitable.
>
> Generally speaking, then, it can be said that poor driving is the root cause of most accidents, although whether this is causing an increase in accidents or whether it is simply the rising number of vehicles on the road that is increasing would involve considerable research.
>
> (256 words)

Unit 9.8 TEST (page 212)

The three graphs present changes in exports and revenue in South East Asia from 1970 to 1995.

The line graph shows three different exports, namely manufactured products, timber and other raw materials. From 1970 to 1975, these three exports rose, with timber increasing most dramatically by $20 million US dollars. From 1975, both timber and other raw materials declined as exports fell from nearly one-third of all revenue to slightly more than one-tenth. (This is also reflected in the pie charts.)

Throughout the period presented, the largest increase in exports was from manufactured products. There was a significant increase in tourism, as the 1975 figure had doubled by 1995. However, this was accompanied by a decline of over one-third in domestic revenue. The remaining named source of income, classed as 'other', experienced only a slight increase of 2% over the same period.

In conclusion, it can be observed that while timber and raw material exports fell, revenue from tourism markedly increased.

(161 words)

Unit 9.8 TEST (page 213)

Drug addiction is becoming an increasing problem. In order to reduce this problem, anyone caught using drugs should be automatically sentenced to time in prison. Do you agree or disagree?

When considering what punishments should be delivered for certain crimes, there are a number of factors that need to be considered, such as the extent of an individual's involvement in drugs – as I will now explain.

Drug addiction can begin for a number of reasons, and although drug abuse is illegal the factors which cause the addiction need to be considered. Young people may find themselves pressured by their peers into experimenting with drugs, or some may even seek the narcotic value of the substance as an escape from a particularly harsh reality.

In such cases, prison is unlikely to offer a true solution to the problem. If the only intention was to remove anyone guilty of a crime from society, then it is temporarily effective. However, if the intention was to deter the person involved, then it is a regressive step.

The solution may lie not in prison but in education and support. By removing the causes that led to the problem, there is the possibility of rehabilitating that person and it is at this point that the extent of the offence needs to be considered. For those whom rehabilitation has not helped, prison may be the only alternative in order to act as a deterrent for future potential addicts. Equally, if the criminal is not only an addict but also a supplier, they should receive the full punishment of the law.

In conclusion, if it can be ascertained that the person caught using drugs has a reasonable chance of being rehabilitated without resorting to prison, then this is the route that should be taken.

(267 words)

Unit 9.11 EXERCISE 1 (page 217)

The line graph shows the changes in three factors affecting students over a ten-week period in an IELTS class.

The most striking point is that at the beginning of the course, students' enthusiasm is almost 100 per cent, whereas confidence and ability are only slightly above 20 per cent. Over the first four weeks, both confidence and ability increase, while enthusiasm declines steadily and continues to do so at a slightly lower rate until the sixth week. Confidence takes a sharp fall but then rises again until week 8, while ability continues to climb. Between weeks 7 and 8, enthusiasm overtakes ability at about 70 per cent, finishing on approximately 85 per cent by the end of week 10. Confidence, however, continues to decline from week 8 ending at slightly less than 10 per cent higher than the level in week 1.

Overall, confidence and enthusiasm are within 20 per cent of their week 1 level by the end of the 10 weeks, whereas ability increases throughout.

(168 words)

Unit 9.11 EXERCISE 2 (page 218)

Attitude is as important as knowledge in a test situation. To what extent do you agree?

Students react in different ways to different pressures, but for many people examinations and tests are a time of nervousness and panic. It is here that it could be argued that these kinds of assessments are not a true test of a subject but of the candidate's character, a point of view I will now consider.

Candidates taking a test with no understanding of the subject are unlikely to do very well. Without understanding what they are being asked to respond to, they are forced to rely only on common sense, presenting an answer that may be correct. In comparison with studious and prepared candidates, it is obvious that the latter would perform better.

However, a counterargument can be made by considering nervous candidates who have little confidence. Such people could find themselves sitting in the test but unable to organise any of their thoughts, finding that the time allotted for the test has gone before having time to write more than a few lines. Now compare the candidates who have written fluently and at length with candidates who have managed only a few lines, and it becomes considerably more difficult to assess whether attitude is as important as knowledge.

Candidates with a confident attitude and others with knowledge of the subject being tested consequently have the possibility of attaining a similar grade. Overall, therefore, what is needed in a test situation is a balance between the two, in which the information gleaned from studying is balanced with a positive and organised approach to the test itself.

(263 words)